Y0-BVP-404

Workers' Participation and Self-Management in Developing Countries

Workers' Participation and Self-Management in Developing Countries

Janez Prasnikar

A15043 610699

Westview Press
BOULDER • SAN FRANCISCO • OXFORD

To my parents

This Westview softcover edition is printed on acid-free paper and bound in library-quality, coated covers that carry the highest rating of the National Association of State Textbook Administrators, in consultation with the Association of American Publishers and the Book Manufacturers' Institute.

All rights reserved. No part of this publication may be reproduced or transmitted in any form or by any means, electronic or mechanical, including photocopy, recording, or any information storage and retrieval system, without permission in writing from the publisher.

Copyright © 1991 by Westview Press, Inc.

Published in 1991 in the United States of America by Westview Press, Inc., 5500 Central Avenue, Boulder, Colorado 80301, and in the United Kingdom by Westview Press, 36 Lonsdale Road, Summertown, Oxford OX2 7EW

Library of Congress Cataloging-in-Publication Data
Prašnikar, Janez
Workers' participation and self-management in developing countries / Janez Prasnikar.
p. cm.
ISBN 0-8133-8172-X
1. Management—Developing countries—Employee participation.
I. Title.
HD5660.D44P73 1991
658.3′152′091724—dc20 90-26929
CIP

Printed and bound in the United States of America

The paper used in this publication meets the requirements of the American National Standard for Permanence of Paper for Printed Library Materials Z39.48-1984.

10 9 8 7 6 5 4 3 2 1

CONTENTS

List of Tables and Figures viii
Foreword, Jan Svejnar x
Acknowledgments xi

Introduction 1

Notes, 2

1 The Overview of Theoretical and Empirical Literature Concerning Worker's Participation and Self-Management 3

Theoretical Findings on Worker's Participation and Self-Management, 3
Industrial Sociology and Industrial Democracy, 3
Basic Findings of the Economics of Self-Management, 6
Contemporary Political Movements in Participation and Self-Management, 13

Participation and Self-Management in Contemporary Societies, 15
Workers' Participation and Self-Management in Capitalist Countries, 15
Participation and Self-Management in Socialist Countries, 18
Participation and Self-Management in Developing Countries, 18
Notes, 19

2 The Evolution of Workers' Participation and Self-Management in Some Developing Countries 23

The Model of Transition into Self-Managed Societies in Developing Countries, 23
Basic Motives for the Introduction of Participation and Self-Management in Thirteen Countries, 25
Degrees of Development, Forms of Ownership and Workers' Participation, 35
Notes, 46

3 Institutional Structure of Participation and Self-Management in Developing Countries 49

Algeria, 49
Bangladesh, 50

Bolivia, 51
Costa Rica, 52
Guyana, 53
India, 53
Malta, 54
Mexico, 57
Peru, 58
Sri Lanka, 59
Tanzania, 60
Yugoslavia, 60
Zambia, 63
Notes, 63

4 Practice of Participation and Self-Management in the Developing Countries Under Study 67

Basic Characteristics of Firms and the Degree of Formal Participation, 68
Real Participation and Self-Management of Workers in Decision-Making in Selected Enterprises, 76
Are Workers Really Participating in Adopting Key Decisions in the Selected Enterprises? 76
Direct and Indirect Management of Workers in the Selected Enterprises, 87
The Role of Management in Decision-Making, 95
The Relation of the Unions to Workers' Participation and Self-Management in the Selected Enterprises, 100
The Views of Workers About the Attained Degree of Participation and Self-Management, 103
Fundamental Findings About Economic Behaviour of the Selected Enterprises, 111
Productivity and Technology, 111
Employment Policy in Selected Participatory and Self-Managed Firms, 113
Internal Rewards of Workers in the Selected Participatory and Self-Managed Enterprises, 116
Financing of Enterprises Under Review, 125
Entry of New Enterprises into the Market Structure, 128
Notes, 129

5 Conclusions 137

References 143
Index 150

TABLES AND FIGURES

Tables

2.1 Foundations of Participation, Legislation, Proponents and Their Motives 26
2.2 Stages of Development, Character of Ownership, Extent and Degree of Participation 36
4.1 Basic Features of the Enterprises Under the Research 70
4.2 Actual Degree of Workers' Participation and Self-Management in the Selected Enterprises 80
4.3 Direct and Indirect Workers' Management 88
4.4 The Role of the Management and Its View on Participation and Self-Management 96
4.5 The Relation of Unions Toward Participation and Self-Management 101
4.6 Opinions of Workers on Participation and Self-Management 104
4.7 An Overview of the Schemes of Fringe and Welfare Benefits in the Enterprises 117

Figures

3.1 Organizational Chart of the Management Bodies in the Industrial Enterprises in Algeria 50
3.2 Organizational Structure of the Management in COMIBOL 51
3.3 Organizational Structure of the Productive Cooperative in Costa Rica 52
3.4 Structure in Management in Guyana 54
3.5 Workers' Managers, Shop Councils and Joint Councils in India 55
3.6 Self-Management Bodies in Malta Drydocks 56
3.7 Organizational Chart of the Management Bodies in the Productive Cooperatives in Mexico 57
3.8 The Structure of the Management Bodies in the Public Enterprises in Sri Lanka 59
3.9 Management Bodies in Industrial Enterprises in Tanzania 61
3.10 The Structure of Management in the Yugoslav Self-Managed Enterprise 62

Schemes

4.1 The Relation Between Workers' Welfare, Secondary Objective, Decisive Variables and Decisive Groups 78

FOREWORD

This book represents an extremely valuable contribution to our understanding of an important subject — the extent, form and merit of workers' participation in management in developing countries. While the theoretical literature on the subject of workers' participation is relatively advanced and a number of empirical studies exist in individual developed and, to a lesser extent, developing countries, this is the first comprehensive study of a large number of developing country cases within a broad, interdisciplinary framework.

Drawing on his background as an economist and a specialist on the Yugoslav system of workers' self-management, Janez Prasnikar has analyzed an extraordinary amount of dispersed information on the experience with workers' participation in thirteen developing countries. He has embedded the cases into a theoretical framework, drawing on the economic and sociological literatures. In the case studies the author discusses the institutional structure of participation in the diverse country settings. The cases are followed by an analysis of the major issues raised with respect to the existence and functioning of the participatory systems. The concluding section summarizes the main findings and policy conclusions.

This book is invaluable for all students of participatory and self-managed economies.

Jan Svejnar

ACKNOWLEDGMENTS

I wish to thank the many people who contributed to this book. Special recognition goes to the founders and supporters of the research project, "Workers' Self-Management and Participation in Decision Making as a Factor of Socioeconomic Changes and Economic Development in Developing Countries," and to the associates at the International Center for Public Enterprises (ICPE) in Ljubljana who executed the project. Without their dedication it would have been impossible to collect the extensive data explored here. Ales Vahcic guided and supervised the project and spent much time in organizing the collection and the analysis of the data. Vesna Smole-Grobovsek did secretarial work on the project. There are, of course, many others whose work cannot be identified in this book, but who provided substantial help during the research project.

I am especially grateful to Jan Svejnar and the Economics Department at the University of Pittsburgh, as well as to Jaroslav Vanek and the Program for Participation and Labor Managed Systems at Cornell University, where I wrote most of this book. It was a great opportunity to work with them and to use the facilities of both universities.

I wish to acknowledge additional thanks to my wife, Vesna, and to Robert Utman, who did most of the translation; I also thank Lauree Graham and Marinka Smodis for invaluable help in the preparation of the manuscript.

All errors that remain in this book are mine.

Janez Prasnikar

Introduction

This book is a summary of "*Workers' Self-Management and Participation in Decision Making as a Factor of Socioeconomic Changes and Economic Development in Developing Countries*," an international research project which focused on issues of participation and self-management in several developing countries.[1] The project was completed in three phases. In the first phase the focus was on the identification of the first stages of active participation and self-management in the developing countries under study.[2] The objective of the research project was to analyze the history of the introduction of workers' participation and self-management and the incentives involved. The results of the first phase of the study were published in *Workers' Self-Management and Participation in Developing Countries* (Sethi, K. 1983).

In the second phase of the project, research focused on the analysis of participation and self-management in the developing countries under study. The analysis involved the participation process and self-management, both on the global level and the enterprise level. In this case nine country syntheses were published in three publications of the ICPE. Several case studies were also produced and published in the three subsequent ICPE issues. The last phase of the project represented the comparative study of the results from the first and second phases of the project.[3]

In Chapter 1 we derive the basic theoretical results from the field of self-management, and participation within the framework of industrial sociology, the economics of self-management and that part of political science which deals with aspects of participation and self-management. In Chapters 2 and 3 we present the basic findings of the comparative analysis of the processes of participation and self-management in the countries under study. In Chapter 4, we summarize the basic findings of the research.

Notes

1. The idea for this project came out at the fourth conference of the leaders of the nonaligned countries in Algeria (September, 1973) with the intent to investigate the problems of introducing self-management and participation in the developing countries and to offer suggestions for effective implementation. The formal constitution of the project in which nine developing countries took part was made in May 1976. Organization of this project was undertaken by The International Center for Public Enterprises (ICPE) in Ljubljana with the cooperation of The Institute for Social Studies in Hague.

2. The countries included in this study are: Algeria, Bangladesh, Bolivia, Costa Rica, Guyana, India, Malta, Mexico, Peru, Sri Lanka, Tanzania, Yugoslavia and Zambia.

3. The following comparative studies are used: M. Glas, Monograph in the Economic Issues (1986); B. Kavcic, Workers' Participation and Self-Management: The Sociological Approach (1986); N. Mugendi, Workers' Participation and Self-Management: Its Politics and Comparative Perspectives (1986); V. Stambuk, Filozofsko-socioloski aspekti samoupravljanja in participacije (1986); K. Sethi, Workers' Self-Management and Participation and Structure and Process of Work Organizations and Industrial Relations (1986).

1

The Overview of Theoretical and Empirical Literature Concerning Workers' Participation and Self-Management

Theoretical Findings on Workers' Participation and Self-Management

Industrial Sociology and Industrial Democracy

Theory of Industrial Democracy. Recently there has been increasing interest in the concept of industrial democracy. Outmoded organizational theories[1] have tended to be replaced by newer theories, which are based upon the idea that human beings must be an active element in the production process. This viewpoint is reflected in The Human Relations Theory, which is based on the categorization of human needs as expressed in Maslow's writing, where work is considered a fundamental human need that must be taken into account in improving working conditions and working relations. This theory suggests that workers should be included in the management decision-making process. The Human Relations Approach is the key for improving motivation and developing each human being's greatest potential.[2] Socio-technical Theory and Job Redesign[3] established that workers' participation is a crucial element in increasing workers' trust in management and decreasing their alienation — thus increasing their motivation and economic efficiency. Both approaches sought to demonstrate that more harmonious relations between workers and capital, along with a general increase in social welfare,[4] would result from the increase in worker's participation in management.[5]

Contrary to the theory of limited participation, or partial control, the theory of self-managed decision-making[6] considers the removal of the hierarchy in the political sense — a result of introducting equal rights for workers. However, the hierarchy is still maintained within the technical division of work. This theory employs self-management as a means for decreasing alienation, while building a freely managed society in which each person can develop his or her personality.

Forms of Workers' Participation. Clarke et al.[7] distinguishes between participation concentrated on work tasks (work-centered participation) and participation concentrated on the distribution of power (power-centered participation). The former is described by the Human Theory Approach. The latter is focused on the control of workers in decision-making and in the distribution of power.

Bernstein outlines the degree of workers' control and the forms in which control is executed.[8] He distinguishes between four degrees of participation. At the lowest degree of participation, workers merely provide written or oral suggestions, which are later reviewed by management. Management can ignore or act on these suggestions. The second form involves discussion between workers and management. The workers have the right to be informed, to discuss their interests, to protest, and to offer suggestions through employee coinfluence. However, the management structure still makes the final decisions. The third form is joint management, or co-determination, in which both of the parties have the right to veto decisions or form joint-decision committees. The most advanced form is self-management, which provides for the full participation of all of the members of the firm, with workers having total control over decision-making. Vanek (1971)[9] develops six characteristics of the self-managed enterprise:

1. There must be total workers' participation in all levels of the organization;
2. All workers have the right to decide how net income will be distributed. There tends to be a higher level of equality in wages among workers in a self-managed firm than there is in a capitalistic firm;
3. The means of production are owned by the workers; are socially owned; or are rented from external institutions (state, union or private owners);
4. The enterprise maximizes the welfare of its workers;
5. Profit, which is the residual after covering all expenses, is kept by the enterprise until the workers decide how to allocate it. The profits can then be distributed to the workers, used for collective consumption, or reinvested;
6. If in a democratic organization the workers rent the capital, a real positive interest rate on borrowed capital should exist. The firm is considered to be a labor-managed firm if the workers pay a capital rent on invested capital to the owners of capital. It is a worker-managed firm if workers do not pay a capital rent in the context of socially owned capital. It is important to distinguish between these two types of participatory enterprises, as each type represents a different form of social ownership.[10] Both types of enterprise as well as the production cooperatives can be put in the same group of self-managed enterprises if they each fulfill the criterion of democratic control by the workers.

Internal Requirements for Feasible Democratic Organization. In order to attain genuine workers' participation in the management of a formally organized democratic enterprise, Bernstein (1976) suggests five requirements:[11]

1. Workers must have adequate access to information. There must exist a mechanism to guarantee a proper flow of correct information;
2. Basic political freedoms must be extended to all workers (freedom of speech, security in complaining, secret voting, a fair defense in legal cases, the right to dispute job displacement). Organizational by-laws must be accepted by a two-thirds majority of the workers. Finally, political freedom should be a long term goal and guarantee of this type of society;
3. Independent judgement must be provided to secure the rights of individuals. Judgement must work in accordance with the rules which guarantee justice, guarantee the basic individual rights of workers and ensure that the firm's activity follow the organizational bylaws;
4. Confidence must be built into participation and democracy. In this respect the following must be avoided: rigidity of thought; indifference; emphasis on extreme loyalty; intransigence; and excessive short-term orientation. It is important to develop an environment which encourages freedom of thought and creativity;
5. All workers must participate in making decisions about income distribution with additional income offered as a bonus payment. As a motivational factor, the bonus must be directly related to work done; distributed according to the written bylaws (otherwise there may be manipulation of the distributions); available to all workers, (otherwise there may be workers' segregation); separated from personal income and can be paid in the form of collective consumption of workers. The amount of the bonuses is the ultimate recognition of the workers' success.

However, Bernstein and others have discovered that formal ownership is not related to the degree of worker participation in decision-making.[12] Rather, the package of rights that workers possess in the enterprise determines their level of participation in the decision-making process.

Advantages and Disadvantages of Democratic Organization. Industrial sociology analyzes the advantages of the democratic organization when compared to the traditional hierarchical firm. Because of the collective spirit of the democratic organization, there is a marked increase in the motivation of workers, the probability that workers will develop themselves in other fields as well as a decrease in the need for control and internal competitive behavior. These characteristics of democratic decision-making lead to decreased conflicts and absenteeism, which in turn lead to increased economic efficiency. In addition to economic efficiency, democracy in decision making decreases alienation and fosters the development of the following altruistic values: social welfare (sufficient employment, environmentally sound ventures); production of socially valuable goods; and fulfillment of collective needs of workers (collective consumption for cultural enrichment, recreation, etc.).[13]

The literature on industrial sociology highlights the various problems associated with the implementation of democratic management:

1. The length of time needed to make decisions in democratic organizations is greater than that which is required in hierarchical ones;
2. Democratic organizations require a higher degree of homogeneity than do hierarchical institutions. This is especially true if the cooperative enterprise is located in a nondemocratic environment;
3. Restrictions in the organization are especially pronounced when the functions of self-management and control (day to day management) are not suitably separated.[14] In these cases the question of accountability arises. Moreover, difficulties arise as a result of the fragmentation of members and of the acceptance of inconsistent decisions;
4. Factors such as the lack of motivation for making democratic decisions and the lack of knowledge which limit members' capabilities to choose individual paths of development and values hamper the successful growth of democractic forms;
5. Based on individual relations between members, democratic management may increase the volatility of personal emotions and thus lead to conflicts which are difficult to overcome; and
6. The possibility exists that individuals or groups of individuals will manipulate the decision-making process for their own benefit.

Basic Findings of the Economics of Self-Management

The breadth of literature on the working of self-managed enterprises is so wide that it is impossible to introduce it all in this short volume. Therefore, the focus of this study shall be limited to the three basic categories which present the heart of the discipline of self-management: economic efficiency of self-managed enterprises; sufficiency of the self-managed national economy; and empirical findings on the nature of the working of self-managed production units.

Findings on the Efficiency of Self-Managed Enterprises.[15] The aforementioned potential reasons for the inefficient operation of self-managed enterprises are not the sole focus of the economics of self-management. This economic theory develops a much more elegant way of explaining cooperative production. Instruments which were developed in neoclassical theory for analyzing the efficiency of the capitalist firm are employed to analyze self-managed firms. However, in the case of the self-managed firm, the maximization hypothesis is transformed: instead of maximizing profits the firm maximizes net income per worker. Moreover, it establishes the framework for the comparison of efficiency between self-managed and capitalistic enterprises.

This analytical framework was first developed by Ward in his famous article in 1958. In this study he discovered the perverse response of the self-managed firm to changes in market parameters. In his model of the Illyrian firm, an increase in the product price leads to a decrease in employment and production. On the other hand, a decrease in the product price leads to an increase in employment and production. Self-managed firms therefore respond differently to price changes than do capitalistic firms. Later it was discovered (Meade, 1972) that optimal economic allocation does not arise in economies in which firms are earning different incomes, because workers in high-paying enterprises will not admit workers from low-paying ones. In addition, assuming that self-managed enterprises are financed internally, there will be less investment (and therefore less growth) than in capitalistic enterprises (Furobotn, 1979). These results of the comparison of efficiency between self-managed and capitalistic enterprises prove that the self-managed firm and the self-managed economy are less efficient than the capitalist alternatives.

It was soon recognized that the above conclusions are based on the assumption on which specific models are built. Instead of using the very simple model of a self-managed firm in which there is only one variable factor and only one product (Ward's model), one can use a more complicated model of a self-managed firm in which more variable factors and products are involved. Moreover, if group solidarity exists, the cooperative firm can collectively decrease the number of hours worked instead of laying off workers. Furthermore, taking compensation for workers who leave a self-managed firm becomes more efficient as it was assumed in the pioneering models.[16]

An active branch of economic theory has grown out of the discussions on the efficiency of the self-managed firm. However, there is a great deal of literature which can be classified as too abstract for use in the real analysis of contemporary world events. Because of this, we will not delve to deeply into a discussion about whether or not the self-managed firm is more efficient than the capitalist firm. However, a theoretical discussion about the behavioral responses of the self-managed firm is not without use in the understanding of the operation of this type of enterprise in the real world. At least four topics[17] address new questions which are important for understanding the results of workers' participation and self-management in the real world. Therefore these topics will be analyzed in more detail.

Employment Policy of the Self-Managed Firm. The first models of the self-managed firm (Ward 1958, Domar 1966, Vanek 1970) explicitly assumed that the firm responds to certain changes in market parameters by varying the number of workers employed. In the last few years the theory has focused on more practical questions, such as what can be done if market conditions require a decrease in production and employment? How can the firm increase the number of employed workers without damaging efficiency? In studying these problems, Horvat (1986) explained that workers in a self-managed firm hire capital and do not fire fellow members. If market conditions deteriorate, the workers decrease the number of hours worked or produce for inventory purposes. If market conditions improve, members' working hours are increased or seasonal workers are employed. However, Horvat's assumption is that it is always possible to find technology which preserves the competitiveness of the firm, while maintaining employment of an equal or even increasing number of workers. Yet, they may have to quickly adjust employment due to a decrease in demand, which requires closing the production line. What can be done in this situation? Which workers should stay and which should leave the firm? The literature on the subject suggests different possibilities. Meade (1972), for example, suggests that younger workers should exchange employment today for continuous employment later, which they will obtain when they are older. Steinherr and Thisse (1979) support the idea of randomly selecting workers to leave the firm in such a crisis. Bonin (1984) and Spinnewyn and Svejnar (1990) analyze the method of compensating workers who leave the firm. If the workers who stay in the firm compensate the workers who leave the firm in the amount of the difference between the income offered in the first and the second firm, the self-managed economy can maintain its macroeconomic stability (Spinnewyn and Svejnar 1990).

The same problem is addressed when hiring new workers. From praxis we know that when market circumstances require the increase of production, the majority of self-managed firms hire seasonal workers. Because of the potential profit earned, it becomes very attractive for the firm to operate in this manner. However, the danger exists that the self-managed firm will become a capitalist firm (Ben Ner, 1982). It is also known that in times of crisis, self-managed enterprise systems, such as those in Yugoslavia and Mondragon, do not hire new workers. (Estrin, 1985). There is also a serious problem involving the employment of new members in self-managed firms in regions with high unemployment.[18] How can the self-managed firm employ larger numbers of workers? Domar (1966) suggested that the firm pay differential wages for equal work. This, of course, destroys the nature of self-management. Vanek (1970) stressed the entry of new firms into the market structure. A special supporting organization would deal with the entry of new firms. Spinnewyn and Svejnar (1990) stressed the bargaining of unemployed workers with employed workers in self-managed firms. If one takes into account the various preferences of workers of different generations, these bargaining processes lead to a higher degree of employment in a self-managed firm than is predicted by simple models.

Internal Rewards of Workers in a Self-Managed Firm. A self-managed firm provides internal rewards on a more egalitarian basis than does a capitalist firm. Besides the existence of funds which are used for collective consumption such as housing and vacation facilities, self-managed firms are also characterized by smaller differences in the personal incomes of their members than those in the capitalist firms.

Two questions thus arise. How does egalitarian distribution influence the incentives of workers? And, how can individual preferences between the leisure and work of each worker be included in collective goals?

First, it can be said that the problem of egalitarian distribution and workers' incentives arises especially in times of crisis when special groups of workers with specific skills demand higher wages.[19] At that time it is very difficult for members to agree on the new proportions between different pay scales, as the decision involves all of the workers in the firm. One possible solution for the firm is to hire these types of workers as they would hire any other input in the competitive market.[20] However, in a self-managed national economy, it is necessary to develop some kind of labor market. The difference between the lowest income and the highest income in this case should be adjusted to social and tax policies.

Frequently, existing literature highlights two problems which are observed in reality and which are related to the second question.[21] If the pay scale is built in an egalitarian way, by instituting the division of income according to needs or by establishing equal income for everyone, the free-rider effect arises. No individual is required to make any special effort to receive income. But if the remuneration of workers is based on the number of hours worked (the more one works, the higher his or her pay will be), high income differences (if some workers do not work as much as others) or the increase of work over the optimal level (if too many workers work excessively) can result. Sen (1966) suggests that the adjustment of both systems (division by needs and division by work) should be used in accordance with practical experience.

Financing of a Self-Managed Firm and the Division of Risk. In reality there exist self-managed firms such as production cooperatives, with various financial structures: debt owed to the members of the firm or to external institutions; joint equity by the members of the firm; social ownership or equity of external institutions. These distinctions lead to the important debate between the advocates of internal financing of the self-managed firm and the advocates the external financing of the self-managed firm. The discussion raised by the advocates of the so-called "property rights theory" (Furobotn, Pejovich) who adopted the Yugoslav concept of social ownership in which workers save from the retained earnings and reinvest in a firm. The aforementioned authors stressed that when workers have no claims on the residual income, they redistribute the residual income into personal incomes and personal bank accounts. Opportunity costs of investment are very high in such cases and total dependence on bank financing is the result of existing ownership rights. The consequence is the inefficient allocation of capital along with chronic inflation (Furobotn, 1970, 1979). But even in the case of external (bank) financing, a self-managed firm invests less than does a capitalist firm. If firms need to maintain the real value of capital,[22] or to increase it, they will invest, provided they need not repay the principal (Bonin, 1984). If they must repay the principal, they will, in effect, be taxed twice because they must pay depreciation which is then applied to the maintenance of the capital and the principal. (Zafiris, 1982).

On the other hand, Stephen (1978) proved that the difficulty of financing self-managed firms does not exist if there is a totally developed capital market and if the repayment of the loan is adjusted to the calculation of depreciation. Also, he showed that negative results are diminished if banks refinance the debt of the firm (rolling over credit). However, it is also important to remember that workers will not fire themselves (see Horvat's counter-argument, 1986). If the tax on income from interest in a self-managed society is correctly calculated, workers will save in firms and thus, the self-managed firm will invest as much as does the capitalist firm.

This discussion, however, does not provide a final answer to the question of financing a self-managed firm. Findings in finance theory reveal that there is a limit to external financing which is connected to the division of risk. Meanwhile, the limits of internal financing are connected to the efficiency of investment. As a result, it is important to conclude that neither total external financing nor total internal financing leads to optimal results. Thus, the argument for the partial external and partial internal financing of self-managed firm consists of two parts. The first relates to the self-managed firm which operates in the context of capitalism; the second relates to such an enterprise which operates in a developed self-managed society. These arguments will be discussed respectively.

Dreze (1976) discovered that, in the framework of capitalism, it is difficult to find suitable ways to finance self-managed firms so that they will operate efficiently. Accordingly, he sees a low probability that workers would invest in their firm because of the large risks involved. An individual's investment in a self-managed firm is solely held in that one enterprise, precluding any hedge investment. It would obviously be preferable to spread one's funds into several investments, a common way of spreading risk in capitalism. Another possibility is to invest in a savings account thereby completely avoiding all risk. Gui (1985) discovered that banks and other investors (on the basis of non-voting shares) would not invest in self-managed firms because of the lack of control over the internal decision-making process of the firm. Workers can opt for policies which may drastically change the profitability of the firm and increase the possibility of bankruptcy after signing any contracts with external investors. For the external investors, the amount of workers' savings in the investment project (self-financing) indicates the degree of risk that the workers are willing to undertake. It is therefore much more appropriate for the workers to save (via self-financing) than to be entirely dependent on the capital market. But, it is also evident that in this case workers necessarily bear a higher risk in investing in a self-managed firm than they would in a capitalist one.[23]

These similar principles are still relevant to the developed forms of self-management as in Yugoslavia or Mondragon, but they will be explained somewhat differently. Total external financing is undesirable because the entire capital risk must be undertaken by the State.[24] This gives the State control over the allocation of capital. On the other hand, total internal financing is equally undesirable because of the inefficient allocation of capital that it causes and the problems of insufficient accumulation within these firms. A possible solution to this problem is the use of a combination of the internal investment of members (equal shares for all members), collective reserve funds (self-financing) and bank financing (external financing). Banks are able to take the funds of individuals and spread the investment of these funds over several areas, bearing risk jointly with firms.[25] Another suggestion is made by Vanek (1977) and McCain (1977) who propose that a participatory bond can be used as a way to finance self-managed enterprise. But this case involves joint decision making between internal and external investors rather than a pure model of the self-managed enterprise.

Entry of New Firms into Market Structure. Vanek (1970) develops the thesis that the entry of new firms is a very important element concerning the efficiency of a self-managed economy. Because the self-managed firm operates in the range of constant returns to scale, it is usually smaller than its capitalist counterpart. On the other hand, members of self-managed firms earn more income than do employees of capitalist firms. With the entry of new enterprises into the market, it is important that, in the long run, the same range of production can be reached in the self-managed economy as in capitalism. Moreover, all rental incomes will be eliminated. Due to this fact, the entry of new firms is a crucial element in the dynamics of supply and demand, the reduction of monopoly power and the fostering of entrepreneurship. Estrin (1983) further developed Vanek's argument for the necessity of the entry of new firms. This is elaborated by focusing on the equalization of productivity in various industries and the reduction of income differentials.

Macroeconomic Stability of the Self-Managed Economy. The literature on the macroeconomics of self-management is small compared to that of the microeconomics. Aside from the work on the institutions of the self-managed economy (Horvat, 1982; Vanek, 1987), there remain only a few attempts at developing formal macroeconomic theory on the self-managed economy. Ward (1967) and Vanek (1970) employed a one-sector model of the national economy. Ward used the classical quantity theory of money; Vanek, on the other hand, used a Keynesian formulation of monetary policy in the model, with firms maximizing income per worker. Later, Vanek (1977) developed the model with the assumption of constant employment and production, which was elaborated by Bradley and Smith (1987), who also developed an open model of the self-managed economy. In general, contemporary macroeconomic theory on self-management is much more controversial than that of microeconomic theory.

Horvat (1982) developed a model of a planned, self-managed market economy based primarily on experiences of the Yugoslav economy. His views on economic activities are based on post-Keynesian theoretical doctrines. Using these tools, he distinguishes between the rules of the plan and those of the market. Vanek (1987) has the same goals in mind for the self-managed economy (growth, egalitarian income distribution, full employment), but bases his model on general equilibrium theory. Contrary to his previous work (Vanek, 1970, 1976) where he defined the self-managed economy as a market economy and Keynesian macroeconomic policy as the means of achieving equilibrium in the national economy, his most recent work (Vanek, 1987) replaces the market with social contracts as a part of social planning. But as has mentioned earlier, all of this is beyond the scope of this paper. In the case of the Yugoslav economy, the assumptions of the above models were never attained and there exists no other environment where one can test the validity of their thesis.

Some Empirical Findings on the Working of Self-Managed Firms. Because more and more empirical research is being done on the working of self-managed firms, there is the danger that one might select certain studies at the expense of other, more important ones. Our selection of the topics is based on the criteria of the practical validity of these results. There are three categories of questions which have special relevance in this regard: the degree of participation of workers on productive efficiency of self-managed firms; the life expectations of self-managed firms; and the reasons behind why there are so few self-managed firms in capitalism.

The Degree of Participation of Workers in Decision-Making and Productive Efficiency of Self-Managed Firms. Earlier, the reasons for the greater degree of efficiency of firms in which participation takes place were discussed. In this regard, Vanek (1970) and Horvat (1982) point out that the high morale of workers leads to greater efforts by workers. Cable and Fitzroy (1980) and Sertel (1982) mentioned that participation decreases conflicts in the workplace and that participating in the decision-making process of income distribution increases the incentives of workers.[26] A great deal of empirical research on Italian, French, English and Israeli production cooperatives has addressed the issue of workers participation and efficiency of self-managed firms. The result can be summarized in the following way:

1. Higher participation of workers in the distribution of profit has a positive impact on productivity. There is also a positive correlation between the amount of equity of workers and the productivity of cooperatives. It is not always clear that a higher degree of participation in decision making leads to higher productivity;
2. In all of the comparative studies of the efficiency of cooperatives and capitalist firms, the cooperatives are not shown to be less efficient;
3. Employment policy is very important in comparing the efficiency of capitalist firms and cooperatives. It has been demonstrated that cooperatives overcome the difficulties of crises more easily than do private firms.[27]

Life Expectations of Cooperatives in Capitalism. The assumption that in capitalism production cooperatives are eventually transformed into private firms is rather inconclusive.[28] There is insufficient data to confirm this belief. However, empirical evidence shows that many cooperatives in reality go bankrupt. The study of French cooperatives[29] indicates that the critical period of survival for the cooperatives is between the third and the fifth year, a time when the cooperatives are usually faced with the lack of financial resources. If the cooperatives survive this critical period, it is possible for them to increase the share of collective reserves in the equity of the firm as well as finance its activity with own funds. The data shows the strong possibility of long-run success for a cooperative with a good internal organization. With regard to the possibility of bankruptcy, cooperatives are no less stable than capitalist firms. Problems that may arise are due less to internal instability than to deficiencies in capital markets which preclude cooperatives from transferring excess funds among themselves.

The Limited Genesis of Cooperatives in Capitalism. Abel (1983) suggests that the risks in capitalism are higher than those in cooperatives, which prevent greater investment in cooperative enterprises. Investment in production cooperatives also limits individuals due to the inefficient nature of joint decision making. Because a capitalistic society stresses egoistic interests and because capital and entrepreneurship are unevenly distributed, it is unlikely that production cooperatives can achieve significant results in the framework of the capitalist order. The only examples of success are found under isolated circumstances as in Mondragon which has its own support organization.

Contemporary Political Movements in Participation and Self-Management

Beginning as a critique of the industrial revolution, the idea of participation and self-management has been connected to various movements towards social transformation.[30] It is interesting to note that almost all socialist revolutions planned some form of a self-managed society. However, the progression of history has led them towards capitalistic or state-controlled orders. Nevertheless, the idea of participation and self-management has been at the frontier of this historical development.

The leading proponents of this idea are found in progressive political parties. For the time being, the countries which formally decided to implement self-management (Yugoslavia, Algeria, Peru, Tanzania), where all of the incentives for development came from top political leaders will not be considered. It will also be assumed that the leading parties of socialist countries have not yet formed their opinions on self-management and participation. Thus it remains clear that participation and self-management play an important role in the ideology of Western European social democratic parties. Elliot (1985) mentions that there exists two schools of thought within the framework of European social democracy: the conservative view that workers' self-management and participation cannot succeed because of fighting between workers and their union representatives; and the liberal view, that participation (cooperation of workers in joint management-labor councils) is an intermediate phase, leading to the development of the democratic self-managed society. However, the empirical reality of the period after World War II demonstrated that the social democratic parties in some countries such as West Germany, Sweden, Norway, Austria and Denmark made remarkable progress in establishing participation and self-management, which drastically changed the relationship between capital and labor. The crises of the seventies focused their attention on unemployment and the preservation of reasonable living standards for workers. Meanwhile, they lost their dominant role in political life. In spite of this, the conclusion should be drawn that the progressive parties can have a powerful impact on the introduction of workers' participation in circumstances of parliamentary democracy.[31]

The discussion will now focus on another important element of this idea reserving for later the discussion of political parties while advance self-managed and participation in developing countries. Again, attention will be focused on the existing practices of unions in the developed capitalist countries, because heretofore, the unions have not played an important role in real socialist countries. In developing countries, unions are either poorly developed or follow the practice of unions in developed capitalist countries or socialist countries.

Theoretically, the unions joined workers for the purpose of collectively gaining shared interests. Modern capitalism established the form of collective bargaining between unions and management which regulates the level of wages and employment. Historically, unions paid attention to these two questions. Only recently has participation and self-management appeared on the agenda of unions.[32] It is important to stress that not all unions value these arrangements. The basic dilemma raised by self-management and participation for some European unions involve agreements with capital and whether or not they should agree on slow changes. Garson (1977) shows that unions in France and Italy rejected the idea of participation and self-management because they believed this would decrease their bargaining power with capital. Horvat (1982) finds this behavior to be irrational because, by doing this, these unions lose the opportunity to introduce their ideas into the structure of the firms in which the workers are employed. The participation of workers in this case is a factor which decreases alienation and promotes the development of the self-management of workers. Obviously, by introducing participation, the union hierarchy fears loosing its status in relation to both labor and capital. Therefore, some unions are maintaining the status quo while progressive parties and other unions are promoting participation and self-management.

Participation and Self-Management in Contemporary Societies

After a review of the main theoretical findings on the nature of participation and self-management, this study will now focus on the observations of participatory and self-managed production units in the real world. The discussion will not include all of the possible cases. Instead, it will summarize the most important material and reveal the patterns which arise.

Workers' Participation and Self-Management in Capitalist Countries

There are many reasons why various forms of participation should grow faster in developed capitalist countries then in the rest of the world:

1. These countries have achieved a substantial degree of political maturity which emphasizes individuals as active political beings. The transformation of political freedom is expected to spread into economic areas;
2. These countries have been able to provide resources to cover not only basic needs, but also to provide for accumulation for other purposes, including individual self-determination.
3. The division of labor which follows industrial revolutions has actually inhibited the self-realization of workers, which is a necessary requirement for the increase of economic efficiency.

On the other hand, the same reasons can contribute to the slow development of self-management.

1. Self-management and participation requires cooperation between people. High standards of living require the right of individuals to make choices.
2. In capitalism it is possible for most groups of people to benefit from bountiful production, particularly in Western countries. Because of this there are no incentives to change the existing social structure.
3. Preserving the political democracy of these countries is often used as an argument for maintaining all other institutions within a capitalist society - such as the legal structure which is not conducive to the development of workers' participation. However, these political democracies employ workers' participation as a covert way to take away private ownership and political freedom.

Therefore, large changes in these societies cannot be expected; rather only incremental and contradictory efforts will be made. The emphasis should thus be on the development of existing participatory arrangements so that success in these enterprises can breed future success.

Horvat (1982) analyzed three forms of the participation in modern capitalist countries: co-determination, socialization of capital and the operation of cooperatives. As this categorization is acceptable from the point of view of the study, the existing literature will be summarized in the same way.

Co-determination in Western European Countries. McCain (1980) suggests that co-determination is the intermediate form of production between capitalist and self-managed firms. According to this opinion, this form attains a higher degree of stability than capitalist or self-managed firms because it stimulates capitalists and workers to make jointly optimal decisions.

The following question arises: How does codetermination work in practice?[33] Svejnar (1982b) did not find major changes in productivity in these firms after codetermination had been introduced in West Germany. Cable and Fitzroy (1980) found that workers' participation has a positive impact on productivity. Streeck (1984) developed the thesis that workers' codetermination in West Germany leads to greater cooperation between workers. Clegg (1983) advocated that there are no major changes between labor and capital. Finally, Crouch (1983) found that in recent years, codetermination in West Germany has diminished.

Based on these findings, can codetermination still be considered as a phase in the evolution of the developed self-managed society? There is no clear answer. A majority of proponents regard co-determination as the most developed form of social relations between labor and capital,[34] guaranteeing economic efficiency. However, they argue that self-management is not rational. On the other hand, some proponents believe that, in the case of successful co-determination experiments, workers having received greater rewards will press management for greater concessions which will be difficult to deny.

Socialization of Private Capital. In the seventies, there was a great deal of interest in the behavior of unions with respect to the formation of collective workers' funds, which would perhaps lead to the socialization of private capital. Swedish and Danish concepts regarding this differ. The Swedes believed in the formation of collective funds which should be calculated on the basis of the firm's profitability and should be managed by unions on the level of industry or on the level of the entire economy (Meidner's Plan). The Danes believed that individual shares should be equally distributed between all workers and calculated on the basis of wage shares. Money collected in this way should be used by the workers for reinvestment in existing firms. Accordingly, workers gain the right to participate in the decision- making process of the Board.[35]

Both views were formed by unions as suggestions to increase capital accumulation and achieve a more egalitarian distribution of income in Swedish and Danish society. Both proposals were applauded.[36] While progressive parties supported them, these proposals were opposed by conservative parties. They believed that the institutionalization of these suggestions would decrease private investment and economic efficiency while increasing union power and thus endangering political democracy. Political events demonstrate that this will be an extended process of sporadic transition and tension between advocates and opponents of this idea.

Production Cooperatives in Capitalism. That production cooperatives in capitalism are an intermediate form of production between private and social ownership is an old idea in the history of socialist thought.[37] But, until now production cooperatives did not play an important role in real capitalist countries. A greater focus on production cooperatives can be noticed in the last twenty years.[38]

Pryor (1983) mentioned five important reasons for the development of cooperatives in capitalism: cooperatives are developed for altruistic reasons of its members; established for no equity to fulfill their basic needs; established by the state because of its broader social goals (development of specific regions, employment); established by individuals in order to increase the economies of scale; and established so workers can buy the firms themselves when firms go bankrupt. Estrin (1985) adds three additional ways of establishing cooperatives: new development of cooperatives; transformation of private firms; and cooperatives which are established by firms which have gone bankrupt.

The main characteristics of production cooperatives in developed capitalist countries are outlined as follows: Usually, cooperatives are small or medium-sized and operate in typical industries, such as construction, printing, furniture and textiles. Abel (1983) highlighted three basic forms of ownership: cooperatives which are externally financed;[39] self-financing cooperatives;[40] and stock-financed cooperatives which carry voting rights (capital-labor partnership). Cooperatives usually choose some combination of the above types of financing. Individual contributions toward financing are usually a requirement for gaining membership into a cooperative in the form of individual shares. These cooperatives often form collective funds or acquire capital via financial markets. Production cooperatives distribute profits in the form of bonuses to either all employees or to members only. Some cooperatives may be composed of hired workers, while others only of members. These relations are usually expressed in the written bylaws of the firm.[41]

The development of the cooperative movement on a broader scale is often dependent on the availability of a support organization. For example, Italian cooperatives are more developed than the French while the Mondragon cooperatives are more developed than the Italian. In particular, the Mondragon cooperatives have developed a network of support organizations.[42] If the support systems can solve the problems of financing the cooperatives and the difficulties of entrepreneurship, cooperatives can become a viable movement in the capitalist countries.

But one cannot expect these cooperatives to have enough incentives in developed capitalist countries. Production cooperatives can hardly compete with private firms in the hostile environment of capitalism. Moreover, the legal system of capitalism is not inclined to the cooperative organizations. These firms are therefore always faced with a shortage of capital and entrepreneurship. Nonetheless, knowledge of the experiences of these cooperatives can be widely disseminated in an effort to improve the management of these cooperatives in general.

Participation and Self-Management in Socialist Countries

There is very little data in the literature on self-management in socialist countries. Most of the literature deals with the possibility of the development of participatory forms of production in these countries. Vanek, 1971; Horvat, 1982 and Vahcic and Petrin, 1986, built their own vision of self-management and attempted to justify it in the ways described below.

Because of restricted political democracy (lack of unions and political parties), the further development of society in these countries depends on the communist party. Since the increase of economic efficiency is a necessary condition for maintaining the power of leaders,[43] the decentralization of the economy is a requirement for the increase of economic efficiency. As the development of a socialist society is based on the ideology of the party, self-management per se is put forth as a means to achieve the goals stated above. In countries with highly developed productive factors, there is a greater possibility for the successful introduction of self-management.

This is based on the experiences of Hungary (1956), Czechoslovakia (1968) and Poland (1981), where movements for the introduction of new forms of participation and self-management in firms took place. Recent experiences of the Soviet Union, China, East Germany, Poland and Hungary, however, reveal mixed evidence about the proposed strategy. It is true that the transformation of state enterprises in some kind of self-managed firms is taking place in many cases. However, it is not clear that efficiency of these firms increases over time. Therefore, plans for further steps of the privatization of state enterprises are suggested, and it is best to leave these questions open to the test of time.

Participation and Self-Management in Developing Countries

From all three groups of countries which are discussed in this study, the conditions for the development of participation and self-management in the developing countries are the most unfavorable. Horvat (1982) explained that a high economic maturity and a long-run political tradition are needed to maintain a developed, self-managed society. In contrast, there is neither political nor economic stability in the majority of developing countries. Their development was built on the traditional social structure (the majority of the population being illiterate and living in rural areas) and inherited the economic system of colonialist countries. Vanek (1971) warned that the rarest production factors in these countries are entrepreneurship and education, which cannot be developed in a short time (capital can be borrowed). Therefore, it will take some time before the developing countries are able to compete.

Past experience has proven that self-management and participation should not be first introduced into developed capitalist countries. Today, most advocates of self-management and participation come from developing countries. Not satisfied with the models offered by capitalist or socialist countries,[44] the developing countries are searching for new models, which are often based on self-management and participation. In the first place, they see workers' participation and self-management as a way of implementing their ideology and preserving political autonomy. In the beginning phase of development, it is not a very important element from the economic standpoint; but later, the changing of the existing social and economic structure plays a central role.

Stambuk (1986) pointed out three forms of development of workers' participation and self-management in developing countries: developing countries which built their economic structure on this concept, such as Yugoslavia, Tanzania, Peru and Algeria; ones in which self-management and participation are just a small part of the larger mixed economy, and have the same characteristics as cooperatives in capitalistic countries; and developing countries in which only particular forms of workers' participation and self-management started on their own.

The most important form of development is stated in the first part. However, despite the economic success in the early development of self-management in these countries, there is now little reason for optimism. The macroeconomic indicators over the last few years for these countries indicate that they all face deep economic crises. There are, of course, many reasons for this. What is the role of participation and self-management in this matter? These questions and others will be discussed in the rest of this work. Therefore, this study will continue with a comparative analysis of participation and self-management in thirteen developing countries which is the topic of the international research reported in this book.

Notes

1. See Weber (1947) and Taylor (1947)
2. There are experiments by E. Maja which concluded that the satisfaction of workers is crucial to the success of the firm. It is important to provide good working conditions, workers' welfare and protect workers from punishment. See Blumberg (1973).
3. The most important proponents of this theory are Herbst, Emery, Thorsrud and Wild.
4. ILO (International Labor Office, 1969) lists four goals to be considered during the implementation of participatory programs: to increase workers' self-realization (the development of the workers' personality and their satisfaction with work); to encourage cooperation between workers and capital; to improve working conditions and to improve the distribution of power in decision-making.

5. Likert (1961) offers four possible systems of management: authoritative (based on punishment); well designed authoritative (the manager or work leader is willing to listen to the workers, but the manager makes all final decisions); consultative (the manager consults the workers, but all final decisions are again made by the manager); participatory (workers and management make decisions together). The last option is the most democratic and has the greatest efficiency potential.
6. See Horvat (1982), Kavcic (1986), Stambuk (1986), Vanek (1971).
7. Clarke, Fatchett, Roberts (1972).
8. Bernstein (1982).
9. See Vanek (1971). Similar ideas are suggested by Horvat (1982).
10. Vanek (1971) states that the system with national ownership and labor-managed firms guarantees social ownership. Horvat (1982) suggests that the self-managed form of enterprise in which the means of production are legally owned by society does, however, guarantee an income for the workers, distributed according to work done. Payment of capital rent is not, in this case, a necessary requirement for defining social ownership.
11. Bernstein (1982).
12. See also Vanek (1975); Horvat (1982); Hammer, Stern, Gordon (1982).
13. See Sen (1977).
14. To distinguish between the strategic decisions which are a part of the democratic process, executive tactical decisions, which are made by top management, professional consultation and operational decisions see Horvat (1982).
15. Because the literature deals narrowly with the self-managed enterprise we will, in the following chapters, consider self-managed firms as the basic unit of analysis. This term expresses various forms of production organization in which the rules of democratic decision-making are exercised.
16. A good overview of this problem is found in the following sources: Bonin, Putterman (1986), Estrin (1983), Pryor (1983), Ireland, Law (1982).
17. These are employment, the internal division of income, financing and the division of risk and the entry of new firms.
18. The Yugoslav experience with the subsidizing of these firms did not turn out to be a good solution for this problem.
19. See Prasnikar and Svejnar (1988).
20. In this direction some efforts have been made in Mondragon's system of cooperatives.
21. See Ireland, Law (1982)
22. This was the legal requirement for the Yugoslav firms
23. The experience of self-managed firms in capitalism confirms this fact. Usually the self-managed firms are self-financing because of the difficulties involved in acquiring external funds. These firms, however, maintain just relations within the enterprise. Primarily these firms operate in industries which require little capital and have little opportunity for development (Abel, 1983).
24. See Vanek (1970, 1986).
25. This is done in the Mondragon cooperatives. Gui (1984) pointed out that this structure of financing increases the incentives of the members and prevents even the

most skilled workers from leaving the firm in times of crisis. This type of incident is common in capitalist firms.

26. Jones and Svejnar (1985) summarized the following positive effects of participation and self-management on the production efficiency: (1) because of the democratic environment, there are less conflicts, higher incentives of workers and a higher tendency of workers to be educated. The enterprise in this way increases the efficiency of its human capital; (2) the working spirit is higher and there is no "sabotage;" (3) workers are willing to fulfill the decisions because of the collective spirit. They mentioned that the literature points also the following negative effects: the managerial workers have lower power in decision-making, which leads to laziness; information has to be given to a higher number of non-experienced decision-makers thus slowing down decision-making and leading to the wrong decisions; inefficient control; and, lower productivity in a self-managed enterprise because workers are unwilling to accept risky decisions.

27. Estrin (1985) explains four possible reasons for this: (1) collective spirit and high incentives of workers; (2) capability of paying workers a lower wage than capitalist firms pay their employees, defined by union agreements; (3) workers valuing security in employment over higher wages; and, (4) help of local communities in isolated areas and high unemployment zones.

28. Webb S. and B. (1920) discussed the notion that cooperatives, having a tendency to desire higher profit, hire workers and are thus transformed into private firms.

29. See Perotin (1986).

30. For more about this, see Horvat (1982); Vanek (1975) and Warner (1984).

31. In this context West Germany is the most notable example. After the early successes with the introduction of codetermination [the law of codetermination in the steel and mining industries (1951), the law of workers' councils (1952)], the social democratic party succeeded in enacting the law of codetermination in all firms with over 2000 employees (1976). In the eighties, when the social democratic party was no longer the ruling political party, the possibilities for developing participation and self-management were considerably diminished.

32. A typical example of this are the Swedish unions. Until the 1970s, they were recognized for acquiring higher employment and wages for their workers. Recently, the unions have focused their attention on getting control over the decision making process. In 1976, the law of codetermination was enacted and the way to form a system of workers collective fund was defined (Meidner's Plan).

33. The greatest efforts for codetermination have been made in West Germany (Codetermination Laws of 1951 and 1976; Works Constitution Acts of 1952 and 1972). Sweden adopted codetermination in 1976. Attempts towards this were also made in Norway, Italy, France and Great Britain, but the economic crises of the 1970s slowed down the development of these forms of production.

34. See McCain (1980).

35. Horvat (1982) suggested that the Danish method should be used for developing countries; the Swedish method should be used for developed capitalist countries. The former is technically simpler and ideologically clearer. In the latter, the speed of the socialization of capital is positively related to profitability.

36. See Ohman (1983).

37.This thesis can be found in Marx and J. S. Mill.
38. See Jones (1978) and Estrin, Jones and Svejnar (1987) about the cycles of the establishment of new cooperatives in Western Europe. For a good survey of cooperatives in the USA, see Jones (1979).
39. Funds can be borrowed from their own members, external institutions (banks, state sources) and private sources.
40. This refers to the collective savings of members or financing by the sale of stock, which does not carry voting rights.
41. For a good survey of the characteristics of cooperatives in Western Europe, see Estrin, Jones and Svejnar (1987).
42. Regarding Italian cooperatives, see Zevi (1982) and Jones and Svejnar (1985). The Mondragon system is described in Bradley and Gelb (1982) and Gui (1984). For information on French cooperatives, see Sibille (1982), Defourny, Estrin and Jones (1985), Defourny (1986) and Perotin (1986). English cooperatives are analyzed by Jones (1976), Jones and Backus (1977) and Jones (1982). Danish cooperatives are analyzed by Mygind (1987) and American by Jones (1979), Conte (1982) and Gunn (1984). The synthesis of these findings can be found in Estrin, Jones and Svejnar (1987) and Estrin (1985).
43. The establishment of a true communist society is very far from being achieved. The inefficiency of these economies makes it even more unlikely to arise. See Horvat (1982).
44. See F. Pryor (1987), where he compared Malawi (the system based on private ownership) and Madagascar (the system based on state ownership).

2

The Evolution of Workers' Participation and Self-Management in Some Developing Countries[1]

At the beginning of this chapter it is necessary to mention that workers' participation and self-management in these countries has been developed in different ways as their founders did not use any particular methodology to start them. Therefore, it is important to look at the entire process of the development of workers' participation and self-management in terms of the abstract model. This will be used as the norm against which the real processes of development in these countries will be evaluated. This chapter will therefore first present the model of transition, followed by the analysis of the practice of participation and self-management in these countries.

The Model of Transition into Self-Managed Societies in Developing Countries

Horvat (1982) pointed out that the tendency of developing countries to become independent was often initiated by violent revolutions. The struggle for independence was usually organized by the party which includes progressive groups (intelligentsia, some of the wealthy and rural people, or military groups). The first task that follows revolution is to establish legal order. A revolutionary party can be much more successful than a parliamentary system. A one-party system can more easily overcome contradictions which a newly liberated country faces due to fighting between different ethnic and political groups, or huge differences in incomes.

The next task is to guarantee the efficiency of the economy during such political changes. Usually, countries in question have a traditional agricultural economic system. A particular, well-prepared strategy should be constructed in order to facilitate the transformation of an agarian society into an industrial society. The basic requirement for an efficient transformation in this direction is the promotion of smooth and high economic growth. Key economic planning should be centralized in the first phase to guarantee efficient development. The state should control the basic financing of investment and foreign trade policy. It is also important to allocate the surplus of agricultural products to the economic sectors which are most likely to be the most productive.

The nationalization of productive factors is usually explained by the state's need to fulfill its established goals. Because these countries have dealt with foreign capital before national liberation, nationalization of capital is necessary for the liberation of the country. Usually it is enough to nationalize only large concerns. Pluralism of ownership is therefore a very promising formula in this phase of economic development. Large firms, such as those in mining, transportation, electricity and other industries, are usually state-owned. Parallel to this are private firms, production cooperatives and small self-managed firms, which have replaced inefficient state and private firms or have been established to fill the "black hole" in various parts of the economy. This refers to a heterogeneous economic structure which is far from equilibrium. But at the given moment, the goal is not to reach equilibrium, but to constrain the dynamics of all of these changes. In this respect, it is very important to steer these countries in the direction of participation and self-management on all levels of social organization. As the introduction of new forms of production in private and public firms gives rise to long-run changes in the economy, the newly established self-managed firms and production cooperatives represent the birth of a new society. It is probable that in the first phase, the efficiency in these firms will not be very great. But in time they will be able to overcome the difficulties of alienation. These firms will prove to be the standard of efficiency and independence.

Horvat stresses that the most ineffective element in implementing this scheme is the one-party system. Usually, in the liberation phase, the development of socialism is the main factor which promotes the integration of society. However, the one party system eventually usurps too much power and becomes dictatorial. Nevertheless, at this early stage of development, it is highly likely that even a pluralistic system, or any other kind of system would still generate the same results.[2] Therefore, it is better to rely on an open-minded party, which has independence and the amelioration of social welfare as its goals. In the first phase, the party and government should work together.[3] However, in the second phase, the party and government should handle separate tasks. Government should then institute democratic reforms and adopt the function of directing the economy. The party, on the other hand, should devote time to overcoming historical conflicts which inhibit democratization. This idea will, step by step, lead to the fulfillment of the goals of national liberation. Although democratic reforms sometimes involve huge contradictions, developing countries will have a better chance of succeeding if they introduce them.

Basic Motives for the Introduction of Participation and Self-Management in Thirteen Countries

Basic data about the introduction, proponents and motives for participation and self-management are listed in Table 2.1. None of the cases will be analyzed in detail,[4] rather the information necessary to test the hypothesis of this study will be emphasized.

The first column of Table 2.1, shows that some forms of participation already existed in these countries before the formal laws supporting them were enacted. The data indicates that there were two situations under which participation and self-management were introduced; in countries with a long tradition of union movements such as those governed by England: Bangladesh, India, Malta, Sri Lanka, Tanzania and Zambia; and, the countries with already-existing cooperative movements, mainly in agriculture, such as Algeria, Costa Rica, Mexico, Peru, Tanzania and Yugoslavia. In Bolivia and Malta, the circumstances differed from both of the above situations because of the major role played by the unions in these countries. The unions wanted to institute much more revolutionary changes, including the requirement that management should be put into the hands of workers. Indeed, this was very successful in some important sectors of the economy.[5] It is interesting to note that South American countries such as Argentina and Mexico, had very important union movements, but did not consider self-management and participation. On the other hand, before the formal introduction of self-management and participation, unions in Peru did not exist.

The data shows that the formal introduction of participation and self-management in countries with developed union movements was greatly facilitated by the enactment of laws which defined the relationship between the owners of capital and workers within a framework of industrial peace as in Bangladesh, India, Malta, Sri Lanka and Zambia. Usually enacted before liberation took place, these laws did not include ambitious goals when the introduction of workers' participation was first initiated. These laws typically retained the same form that they had before the liberation of the country as important changes in the strategy of the implementation of participation and self-management had not yet been effected.

The cases in which the development of participation and self-management was introduced spontaneously and later became a wide social movement are much more worthy of investigation. Usually this occurred concurrently with national liberation, or years later when developing countries such as Algeria, Peru, Tanzania and Yugoslavia announced self-management and participation as their particular way of building society. Either immediately or within a few years after the national struggle for liberation, all four countries legally introduced some form of participation or self-management and tried to rebuild the entire economic structure on this basis. It

TABLE 2.1
FOUNDATIONS OF PARTICIPATION, LEGISLATION, PROPONENTS AND THEIR MOTIVES

COUNTRY	ROOTS OF PARTICIPATION	LEGISLATION	PROPONENTS	MOTIVES
ALGERIA	1961: establishment of first participatory bodies by workers	1971: La Gestion Socialiste des Entreprises (GSE), the introduction of participation and self-management in industry 1971*	government and FLN 1962**	1. social (to increase political awareness of workers) 2. ideological (to eliminate exploitation, to redistribute power in economic and political sphere) 3. economic (to actualize planning goals and increase production) 4. political (to liberate)
BANGLADESH	1947: Industrial Disputes Act: Workers' committees in all firms with over 50 workers	After 1972, more intensive discussion, but incomplete strategy of development	government and Awami league 1947, 1971**	1. to improve working conditions 2. to reduce the communication gap between labour and capital 3. to reduce conflicts between labour and capital

BOLIVIA	1952: nationalization of mines and increased interest in participation	1983: Decree No. 19803, formal establishment of self-management and participatory bodies in COMIBOL;	Bolivian Federation of Unionized Mine Workers (FJTMB) and government	1. to incorporate government plans in COMIBOL 2. to involve workers in the development of COMIBOL (central facet of Bolivian economy) 3. to incorporate and consolidate national interests into COMIBOL
		1952*	1825**	
COSTA RICA	1961: Land Settlement Law (parcelling of land and its transfer to peasants, making the distribution of property more egalitarian)	1968: Law on Cooperative Association (establishment of self-managed cooperatives)	government	1. economic (to increase productivity in agriculture, to increase general level of knowledge, to raise employment) 2. social (to form communal life, to establish egalitarian distribution of income) 3. political (to make productive resources available to workers)
		1961* Agrarian Reform	1821**	

(continues)

Table 2.1 continued

COUNTRY	ROOTS OF PARTICIPATION	LEGISLATION	PROPONENTS	MOTIVES
GUYANA	no data	1970: Guidelines of Workers Participation in Management (introduction of participation in public firms) 1961*	government, and political party in power (Peoples' Progressive Party) 1966**	Very few clear goals; remaining goals are more economic than political: 1. to increase productivity, efficiency and satisfaction of workers 2. to facilitate better relations between workers and management 3. to foster better human rights and Industrial Democracy 4. to foster democracy and improve working conditions
INDIA	first beginnings in textile industry (to improve labour/capital relations): Tat Iron Steel Co. (first workers' council)	1947: Industrial Disputes Act (Introduction of Workers' Committees in factories with over 1,000 employees)	government, with the support of Congress Party and other parties 1947**	Non-specified goals 1. to increase productivity, efficiency and satisfaction of workers 2. to facilitate better relations between workers and capitalists 3. to foster industrial democracy

MALTA	first form of participation in 1940's among port workers	beginning of 1950's: government made a proposal legal basis for participation 1962: legalization with the support of Workers' Ordinance)	Government, Labour Party and GWU (General Workers' Union) 1964**	1. to facilitate better relations between workers and capitalists 2. to increase satisfaction of workers and foster greater responsibility 3. to reduce alienation of workers in the workplace
MEXICO	first cooperatives seen in 1870	1939: Law on Cooperatives	depends upon the views of the government in power (especially in periods of social crisis) 1829**	1. to provide alternatives to other production forms during times of crisis 2. to increase productivity 3. to establish broader participatory rights of workers
PERU	mid-nineteenth century: first law on cooperative movement 1891: parliament does not acccept this proposal 1964: law accepted	1969: Juan Valasco Alvarado's program of self-management and participation as a model of Peruvian development	military government with the support of progressive parties and unions 1824**	1. to reform social structures and promote social justice 2. to eliminate exploitation 3. to reform socioeconomic structure (education of workers) 4. to facilitate better relations between workers and capitalist

(continues)

Table 2.1 continued

COUNTRY	ROOTS OF PARTICIPATION	LEGISLATION	PROPONENTS	MOTIVES
SRI LANKA	first form of participation in 1950's	1970: The United Front Election Manifest where the UF decided to implement self-management and participation	government with support of United Front 1948**	1. to increase cooperation between workers and capitalists 2. to improve communication between workers and capitalists
TANZANIA	1962: Nyerere introduced Ujamas villages, the basis of African Socialism; establishment of cooperatives on a regional basis	1964: Security of Employment Act—CAP574 (establishment of workers' committees)	government with the support of party in power (TANU-Tanganyika African National Union, 1967)	1. political: to abolish exploitation through increased socialistic leanings (popular socialism in villages)—popular participation, which should include 90% of population in villages abolish exploitation; workers should manage productive resources 2. to improve education 3. to increase self-motivation and creativity
		1967: nationalization of land after 1967*: nationalization of all productive resources	1969**	4. to increase economies of scale and marketing 5. to facilitate better relations between labour and capitalists and promote industrial peace

YUGOSLAVIA	cooperative movement before WWII	1950: official law transferring state enterprises to workers	government with unions and with the Communist Party	1. political: to abolish exploitation—factories to workers 2. to establish developed socialistic society on a self-managed basis in all areas 3. to establish democratic governing of the economy 4. to incorporate workers' interests—higher economic efficiency 5. to increase education of workers—improvement of working conditions 6. to change the social structure 7. to increase democracy in political life: the struggle against bureaucracy
		1946-48*	1945**	

(continues)

Table 2.1 continued

COUNTRY	ROOTS OF PARTICIPATION	LEGISLATION	PROPONENTS	MOTIVES
ZAMBIA	the beginning of participation in thirties, when workers' committees were established in particular enterprises	1974: The Industrial Relations Act (establishment of workers' councils plants with over 100 employees)	United National Independence Party (president Kaunda—in the framework of the Philosophy of Humanism)	1. to increase (encourage) participation and self-management as a means to achieve liberation and independence from foreign capital Philosophy of Humanism; a. public ownership—transfer of economic power b. egalitarian distribution of wealth c. economy is based on public sector while others are operated under it (mixed economy) d. participatory democracy in industry 2. to foster social justice
			1964**	3. to facilitate better relations between people and the party or government increase efficiency

Legend * nationalization
** liberalization

required a degree of participation between people with different political views because the process of gaining independence was very difficult.[6] Logically, it is highly possible that it was also introduced into the economy. In general, the nationalization of private property, which was introduced after liberation enabled the introduction of some form of participation. Because agricultural production dominated, the first self-managed and participatory organizations were introduced there.[7]

The introduction of self-management and participation in Bolivia and Malta in two firms, COMIBOL and Malta Drydocks, has been discussed above. In Costa Rica and Mexico, participation was strongly supported by the agricultural sector and cooperatives. In Mexico, agricultural cooperatives have a long standing tradition; in Costa Rica, the legalization of agricultural cooperatives was established in 1968, after the agricultural reform of 1961 proved unsuccessful. The intent of the 1968 reform was to increase the efficiency of farming. In Guyana, participation and self-management in state firms was introduced in 1970, following independence in 1966 and nationalization in 1969. However, it is not clear if workers' participation and self-management had any effect on the firms in this country.

The third column of Table 2.1, shows the main proponents of participation and self-management in each of the countries. Because the state and its executive bodies control legislation, the government actually plays the most vital role in the majority of cases. Much more important however, is the question of who initiated the legislation. In the countries under study; such, as Algeria, Bangladesh, Guyana, India, Tanzania, Yugoslavia and Zambia in most cases self-management and participation were established by the parties which struggled for independence and seized political power. This confirms the thesis that all of these ideas were present during a time when the participation of different political groups was required. Eventually this phenomenon spread into the economic sphere. In Sri Lanka, participation was introduced on a large scale when the progressive parties joined the United Front in 1970. In Malta, much more attention was focused on participation when the Labor party was in power. In Costa Rica, participation was connected to the introduction of social programs such as the redistribution of property to the poor, and attempted at starting agricultural cooperatives. In Mexico, the cooperative movements depended upon the particular government in power, especially in times of crisis when it atempts to alleviate current social problems. In Peru, the military government, along with the progressive parties and unions supported self-management and participation. In Bolivia, the main contributing factor to participation was the union of mining workers (FSTMB). Union organization also played a major role in the introduction of self-management in Yugoslavia. In general, the data shows that the introduction of participation and self-management is connected to progressive political parties and unions.

The motives for the introduction of participation and self-management in the countries under study were mainly political. One can distinguish between those countries with a clearly defined political goal of establishing participation and self-management, such as Algeria, Peru, Tanzania and Yugoslavia, and those in which this explicit goal was not formally established. In the latter, participation and self-management were used solely as a political device to satisfy ideological imperatives, as in Bangladesh, Bolivia, Costa Rica, Guyana, India, Malta, Mexico, Sri Lanka and Zambia. Political goals which usually appear with the introduction of participation and self-management can be classified into the following groups:

1. Guarantee of independent socioeconomic development — The majority of countries under study such as Algeria, Peru, Tanzania, Yugoslavia and Zambia were former colonies and considered participation and self-management as an alternative model of socioeconomic development which should preserve independence;
2. Removal of exploitation — Long-run colonial dependence and a high degree of economic division in these societies called for participation and self-management as a means to create a just society with an egalitarian division of wealth and income, and political freedom. Participation and self-management was therefore introduced in: Algeria, Peru, Tanzania, Yugoslavia and Zambia in the aim of establishing social order;
3. Education of people and the transformation of the social structure — Because the countries under study are developing countries with a traditional hierarchical social structure and a large percentage of their population involved in agriculture, the role of education should be emphasized. It can contribute considerably to the transformation of the social and economic structures such as the cases in Algeria, Peru, Tanzania and Yugoslavia;[8]
4. Involvement of workers in decision-making and decrease in alienation in the workplace, such as in Guyana, Malta and Yugoslavia;
5. Development of political democracy — Training workers to identify themselves as equal political beings is fundamental to the development of democratic socialism such as Malta, India, Sri Lanka and Tanzania;
6. Development of self-management as a way of life — To build a harmonious democratic society, it is necessary to consider the opinions of the people regarding the distribution of income (self-management) in political life (a system of delegates), such as in Yugoslavia; and,
7. Elimination of bureaucracy from decision making, as in Yugoslavia.

This, however, does not signify that economic goals were not important in those countries which based their development on participation and self-management. In Yugoslavia, for example, the general opinion was that self-management would lead to higher incentives and economic efficiency; in Algeria, the introduction of self-management was connected to the fulfillment of the society's planned goal to increase production; in Tanzania, the introduction of self-management was understood as a means to stimulate incentives and creativity, improve the market process and take advantage of economies of scale. The introduction of participation and self-management in Zambia was a means of transmitting information from the people to the party and the government. This was thought to lead to higher efficiency. However, this was a part of a larger plan for development and was not, in itself, of singular importance.

In developing countries, in which such goals were vaguely defined, participation and self-management usually appeared in the framework of the theory of industrial democracy. The increase of incentives and the productivity of labor is assumed to be the result of the growing trust between workers and the decrease of alienation, which comprise the essence of so-called socio-technical theory and job redesign. These are the motives for the introduction of participation and self-management in the majority of the countries we have studied such as Bangladesh, Costa Rica, Guyana, India, Malta, Mexico and Sri Lanka. In Mexico, participation and self-management are considered to be alternatives to existing forms of production, especially in times of crisis. Participation and self-management in Costa Rica are of vital importance because of their ability to increase employment. The Bolivian government considered participation and self-management in COMIBOL as a means to implement its own plans and national interests as well as a way to involve workers in this enterprise which represents the most important sector in the country. The workers value self-management for its ideological and political significance.

Very often the motivation for participation and self-management rests on the Human Relations Theory, uniting labor and the owners of capital or management which is the basis of the philosophy of industrial peace. Moreover, it emphasizes the improvement of working conditions, involving workers in management, and promoting the development of each individual as a human being. These are the main points which were found in studies on Bangladesh, Costa Rica, Guyana, India, Malta, Peru and Sri Lanka. In addition to these findings, it was also discovered that participation is considered to be a fundamental rights by workers in Mexico. On the surface, it appears that all these goals are not coordinated. They operate within the framework of existing orders which stress either the development of the private or the public sector, while, from the beginning, not much is to be expected from participation and self-management.

Degrees of Development, Forms of Ownership and Workers' Participation

Varying degrees of involvement and differences in participation existed in the countries under study as a result of the different motives behind introducing participation and self-management. The following is a summary of the data presented in Table 2.2.

Four groups of countries in the phases of development of participation and self-management can be distinguished. The first group of countries represents those which based their vision of development upon the model of self-management. In the cases of Algeria, Peru, Tanzania and Yugoslavia, consolidated efforts were made to install such an economic and political system. The most advanced example of this is, of

TABLE 2.2
STAGES OF DEVELOPMENT, CHARACTER OF OWNERSHIP, EXTENT AND DEGREE OF PARTICIPATION

COUNTRY	STAGES OF DEVELOPMENT	CHARACTER OF OWNERSHIP	EXTENT	DEGREE OF PARTICIPATION
ALGERIA	1963: two government laws on establishing participatory bodies in agriculture	collective in agriculture	entire agricultural sector is organized in 1,000 cooperatives	codetermination of workers and government representatives; tendency for wide-spread participation or self-management
	1971: nationalization of land	state in industry		
	1971: beginning of introduction of self-management in industry			
	1975: independent managing of agricultural cooperatives			
BANGLADESH	1947: Industrial Disputes Act (1960, 69, 73, 80)	private	workers' committees do not have a more important role, only some successful cooperatives	workers' committees have only advisory role
	1972: Labour Policy Statement			
	1980-85: Plan—emphasis on agricultural communes	cooperative		

BOLIVIA	1952: Nationalizations of mines 1964: Introduction of limited participation 1970-71: workers' plan for full participation 1983: formal introduction of workers' participation boards	COMIBOL — public	limited to the COMIBOL	codetermination with the tendency toward self-management
COSTA RICA	1961: Land Settlement Law 1968: Law on Cooperative Associations 1982: Law on Cooperative Associations (establishment of Institute for Cooperative Development)	cooperative; tendency toward social ownership	no data; only in agriculture with 24% population (190,000 inhabitants)	tendency for introduction of self-management in cooperative sector
GUYANA	1969: Public Corporations Act (30 public firms) state	state	public sector (80% of economy)	only limited forms of participation; participation only as a consultative device (employee consultation)

(continues)

Table 2.2 continued

COUNTRY	STAGES OF DEVELOPMENT	CHARACTER OF OWNERSHIP	EXTENT	DEGREE OF PARTICIPATION
INDIA	1947: Industrial Disputes Act 1953: Joint Management Council (53 enterprises in industry)	public	no data about the extent; introduction of participation in private and even more so, in public firms	joint consultation in order to achieve high productivity
	1970: workers' representatives on the executive board in public sector (in 1972, in 14 banks) 1975: enterprises with over 500 employees implemented joint plant council, shop council 1977: workers' representatives in plant and on board of directors (3-tier scheme)	private		

MALTA	1950: legal basis for participation; 1965-67: Malta Drydocks—limited participation (joint consultative committee) 1971: strike at Malta Drydock; agreement with government on joint management 1975: Drydocks Act—council elected by workers as the self-management body	Malta Drydocks—state ownership; managed by workers. Some forms of participation in other state, private and union-owned enterprises Participation in government organization	Malta Drydocks is the main sector of Malta's economy (14,819 employees); after 1971: GWU participate in management of textile mills and private ship building (1977: 18 plants with 1750 employees)	mostly joint consultation with the tendency toward self-management at Malta Drydocks
MEXICO	1939: General Law of Cooperative Societies; development of cooperative sector in agriculture—this depends on the party in power	cooperative	1940: 1527 cooperatives 1952: 400 cooperatives 1976: 1802 cooperatives 1982: 3278 cooperatives	self-management in productive cooperatives

(continues)

Table 2.2 continued

COUNTRY	STAGES OF DEVELOPMENT	CHARACTER OF OWNERSHIP	EXTENT	DEGREE OF PARTICIPATION
PERU	1964: low in cooperatives 1968: program of Juan Valasco Alvarado—self-management and participation as a model of development 1969: agricultural reform; foundation of cooperatives in agriculture	— cooperative co-ownership — workers' owning some shares	1981: 2881 cooperatives 39 labour communities 63 enterprises with social ownership	self-management in cooperatives
	1970's: General Law of Industries; public enterprises and introduction of Swedish method of socialization of capital 1974: Social Property Law; foundation of enterprises in social ownership	transition of private ownership into social ownership (15% of net profit is given to workers for buying shares from private investors, with the limitation that only 50% of total capital can be owned by workers		codetermination in labor communities
	1975: new government favors private sector	social ownership		self-management in socially owned enterprises

SRI LANKA	1970: foundation of workers' councils in public enterprises, government institutions and national committees on the regional basis 1977: workers' committees from 70's cancelled (Employee Council Act 32); only consultive role of workers' council remains	public ownership	1975: 212 workers councils in enterprises, governed by Ministry of Transportation, Industry and Science 1979: 280 workers' councils in 45 enterprises in public sector	only advisory role
TANZANIA	1964: establishment of workers' committees (advisory role) 1967: Arusha Declaration (TANU), development strategy of "own" model of socialism 1970: self-management formally introduced in public enterprises and villages communities; the role of workers' councils is not clear 1977: process of participation is spread to government ministries and departments	public	most of the agriculture sector (ujamaa villages) 1967: 64 public enterprises 1975: 142 public enterprises	Workers' council in advisory role; workers in executive board and management structure (wages, distribution of income) = (employee coinfluence); direct decision-making in village cooperatives

(continues)

Table 2.2 continued

COUNTRY	STAGES OF DEVELOPMENT	CHARACTER OF OWNERSHIP	EXTENT	DEGREE OF PARTICIPATION
YUGOSLAVIA	1950: Basic Law on Governance of State Enterprises and Higher Economic Associations 1957: Transfer of Responsibilities to communities and development of their communal system 1961: beginning of so-called phase of market socialism 1971: phase of so called integral self-management system	social ownership (social sector produces 85% GNP)	1949: experimental workers' councils in more than 200 enterprises 1979: 20,064 BOALS	— direct and indirect management of enterprises by workers—self-management — development of self-management interest groups and delegation of decision making in the field of public choice — development of delegation system on all levels of social life

ZAMBIA	1974: The Industrial Relations Act (introduction of workers' councils became operational for all public enterprises, 1976) 1975: establishment of Department of Industrial Participatory Democracy (program for motivating workers participation, pilot studies) 1983: introduction of unions' representatives in boards of directors (introduced in various state enterprises)	public		60% of economy are state enterprises (agriculture, transportation) or supervised by government (parastate). Participation introduced into state and some private firms.	workers' councils have only advisory role (employee consultation)

course, Yugoslavia. The first experiments in self-management (1950-1960), were followed by the introduction of the market variant of self-managed socialism in the sixties, which stressed the independence of self-managed firms and their responsibility for achieving good economic results. In the early seventies a variant of guild socialism with integrated planning, which emphasized bottom-up planning, was introduced. It was based on the independence in decision making of Basic Organizations of Associated Labor (BOAL) and in local communities. Their planned actions were to be coordinated with other units on the same and higher levels of associations. Competition would be replaced with agreements such as social contracts, which would lead to greater coordination between a country's interests and its economic structure in order to make it competitive with the rest of the world. Algeria's efforts in the area of self-management were modeled after the Yugoslav style of self-management. First, they planned self-management in agricultural cooperatives. Later, they attempted the total reconstruct of management in industrial firms. The Peruvian solution was based on the introduction of agricultural cooperatives, the incremental changes of private firms into worker-managed firms,[9] and the establishment of the social sector of the economy. However, Velasco's heirs did not follow his plan; instead they stressed the development of the private sector. In Tanzania, the main emphasis was placed on self-management forms in communes such as ujamaa villages. Some form of participation was also introduced in public and state firms and in government ministries, but the role of workers' councils was not clearly defined.

The second classification of countries are those which developed workers' participation and self-management in selected areas. These countries are: Bolivia, Costa Rica, Malta and Mexico. In Bolivia, this activity was limited to the mining corporation COMIBOL, which represents 70% of mining production in this country. From the beginning phase in which the mines were nationalized in 1952, to the formal introduction of workers' councils in 1983, COMIBOL progressed through several phases, foreshadowing the establishment of the role of workers in decision-making. In a similar way, the entire transformation of shipbuilding was initiated at Malta Drydocks after 1975 when workers took control of the factory. In Costa Rica and Mexico,[10] the emphasis was on the development of participation in agricultural cooperatives.

The third classification of countries are those in which participation is built based on the philosophy of industrial peace. These countries are India, Sri Lanka and Zambia. India never broke the tradition of making collective agreements between the owners of capital and unions despite its long-standing tradition in participation. Therefore, participation in this case has never led to anything beyond employee coinfluence. Similar experiences were found in Sri Lanka. The role of workers' councils was reduced after 1977. The government precisely defined the fields in which the managers of state firms could consult with workers. The plans for participation and self-management in Zambia were much more profound. After the establishment of the Center for Industrial Democracy in 1975, which designed programs for the active participation of workers and directed the development of participation, the members of the executive board in various public firms became the union's representatives by

1983. But the workers' councils, which became law in 1971, retained only a consulting role.[11]

Bangladesh and Guyana were selected as the countries to comprise the fourth group. The development of participation in private and public firms existed in Bangladesh since 1947. Although this requirement was continually re-established, approval of workers' councils in public firms was evident in 1972 as reflected in the Labor Policy Statement. However, unions did not accept this. In Guyana, instructions for the introduction of self-management and participation in public firms were provided in 1970. But neither these instructions nor the practice clearly defined the form of participation that was actually being employed. In both countries, only rudimentary forms of participation were enforced as a result of the ambiguous definition of the role of workers in participation and self-management. Because of this, workers' participation was denied the opportunity to develop on a larger scale.

Firms which have shown some degree of participation are usually the public firms in Algeria, Bolivia, Guyana, India, Malta, Peru, Sri Lanka, Tanzania and Zambia. In particular cases, the study dealt with private firms in Bangladesh, India, Malta and Zambia while in other cases, with cooperative ownerships in Algeria, Bangladesh, Costa Rica, Mexico and Peru. In Tanzania and Zambia, participation was introduced in some parastatal firms, which are firms in which the state holds more than 51% of the shares. A special role related to the ownership of the firm was found in Yugoslavia and Peru. Yugoslavia adopted the concept of social ownership under the control of the working collectives. After 1974, Peru followed the Yugoslav concept, and legislated the same ownership structure called the social property sector.

In the context of the economic activity during the time of this research, participation and self-management were most developed in Yugoslavia. In 1980, the self-managed sector produced more than 85% of gross national product and employed almost six million people, who were organized in 20,064 BOALs, 14,039 working organizations with BOALs and 4,157 working organizations without BOALs. Since self-management was also introduced into agrarian cooperatives and contractual organizations of associated labor, the extent of the self-managed sector was even greater that the above data shows. After Yugoslavia, Algeria had the next most developed system of self-management. In 1979, the entire agricultural sector was organized into over 1,000 cooperatives and the codetermination of workers was introduced in 57 industrial enterprises with over 300,000 workers. Self-managed production units also exist in Peru, where in 1981 there were 2,881 agricultural cooperatives and 39 firms with a so-called labor community in which the process of transforming private capital into workers shares was started. In 63 firms, the system of social ownership was introduced. In Tanzania, the process of establishing village cooperatives involved the entire agricultural population in the 1970's.[12] The introduction of participation and self-management in public firms and institutions involved 142 organizations. Self-management in Bolivia and Malta represents only mining and shipping sectors.[13] In Costa Rica and Mexico, the emphasis was on agricultural cooperatives. In Mexico, for example, 3,278 agricultural cooperatives were in operation. In India, Sri Lanka and Zambia, the role of participation that was introduced into the public sector and private sector was very limited. In Bangladesh[14] and Guyana, no solid program for the development of participation was ever really made.

The most ambitious plans for the development of self-management were found in Yugoslavia where there was also an attempt to incorporate self-management into public works and into the political sphere (the system of delegates). The developed form of a self-managed socialist society was the basic political orientation in Yugoslavia. In Algeria, a special form of codetermination between workers and the management of state firms was introduced, which gave rise to greater participation and self-management. Until 1975, the vision of self-management was much more emphasized in Peru. In Tanzania, the unique brand of African Socialism prevailed. In COMIBOL in Bolivia and in the Drydocks in Malta, codetermination was introduced along with workers' decision-making. In Costa Rica and Mexico,[15] the development of self-management in agricultural cooperatives was noticed. In India, employee coinfluence, which is the joint cooperation between workers and management in public and private firms, was observed. In Sri Lanka and Zambia, employee consultation existed, where the workers' councils only served a consulting function. However, in Bangladesh and Guyana, the role played by the workers' council in firms was unclear.

In general, the data shows that formal participation and self-management, legalization of statutes, government orders for stimulating participation and self-management, and the establishment of support organizations, have spread rapidly throughout these countries during the sixties and seventies. In the eighties, however, there has been a slowdown in the growth of these areas. The reasons for this will be examined later once participation and self-management in these countries has been discussed in greater depth. However, before this, it is necessary to introduce the institutional structures which form the basis for participation and self-management in the countries under study.

Notes

1. This refers to those countries which are under investigation in this study.
2. Because these countries have little experience with democracy and are faced with major economic difficulties in this early phase, the implementation of so-called pluralistic forms of government at this time probably leads to the same results.
3. Also, there should be a multiplicity of opposing forms of production which will stimulate decentralization.
4. For more information, see the list of monographs used in the preparation of this study.
5. In Bolivia, this role was given to The Bolivian Federation of Unionized Mine Workers (FTSMB), which succeeded in nationalizing The Bolivian Mining Corporation (COMIBOL) in 1958. Mining was the most important sector of the economy. From then on, FTSMB focused, on the struggle for participation and self-management, which

was formally introduced in 1983 after the battle between the workers and the army in the streets of La Paz,

Formally introduced in Malta in the forties, self-management and participation really became a force only after 1971, when, the Malta Drydocks firm fell into the hands of workers after the general strike in shipbuilding.

6. An exception to this is the case of Peru, where self-management was introduced by General Juan Velasco Alvarado, who came to power in 1968.

7. In 1963, Algeria enacted legislation to introduce self-management and participation on farms. Nationalization of farming was completed by 1971. Later in 1971, self-management and participation were introduced in industry. In Peru, agricultural cooperatives were established after the agricultural reforms of 1969. In 1970, participation was introduced in industrial firms, followed by social ownership in 1974 in which workers managed the firms. In Tanzania (1962), President Nyrere constructed the strategy of African Socialism, which was based on village communities (Ujamaa villages) and agricultural production. In 1964, the legislature introduced workers' committees into industry. In Yugoslavia, before self-management was introduced into all state firms (in 1950), collectivization in agriculture had taken place but had not produced any results.

8. A typical example of this is found in Tanzania under the presidency of Nyrere in his construction of African Socialism. This country faces the problem of illiteracy in its agricultural population, which comprises 90% of the entire population. According to his opinion, the introduction of participation at all levels of social life (village communities) is a necessary requirement for the change of traditional economic and social structures of the country.

9. This is based on the Swedish method of the socialization of private capital. Fifteen percent of net profit was used for buying shares from shareholders which were then transferred to workers. The workers were, however, unable to acquire more than half of the firm.

10. In Mexico, the concrete industry (Cruz Azul), which employed 1,396 workers, played the same role, yet it represents the entire commune system, consisting of more than 6,000 people.

11. In this context, it is important to note that the requirements for the active role of workers' councils and participation were initiated by private and parastate firms more often than by public firms.

12. It must be pointed out that the agricultural population was organized into compounds comprised of 300 to 400 families.

13. However, there are other instances of workers participation and self-management in the Maltese economy besides Maltese shipbuilding. After 1971, the General Workers Union included self-management in some textile firms and other private shipbuilding firms in 1977, (there were 18 firms organized in this way with a total of 1,750 workers). Profit sharing was introduced into some private firms, such as in Villa Rossa Hotel and Marsa Shipyard. The government introduced partial participation in some departments, for example is the educational sector and, in some of the public firms, the workers were organized into the so-called management committees.

14. In the later years, the emphasis was on agricultural cooperatives.

15. In this context, we will again mention the concrete industry (Cruz Azul), which was more advanced than other firms.

3

Institutional Structure of Participation and Self-Management in Developing Countries

At this point, the study will analyze the extent to which the organizational and legal structures are conducive to the development of participation and self-management in each of these countries. The most effective way to understand this is to investigate different institutional structures in the participative and self-managed firms of each of these countries and their function in decision-making. Because the differences in the legal and organizational structures of these countries are so vast, they will each be discussed separately.

Algeria

It was assumed that agricultural cooperatives in Algeria would be managed by the workers and that industrial management would interact with the state and amalgams of workers (codetermination). In this manner, this type of governance was conducive to the promotion of participation and self-management. Nowadays, in the agriculture sector, the most important branch of the internal structure is the General Assembly of Workers which elects a workers' council and an executive board. In the industrial sector, firms are governed by executive boards, consisting of a general manager chosen by the state, advisors and two representatives of the workers; the Assembly of Workers, which meets twice a year; and five commissions which are named by the Assembly.

Figure 3.1 presents a model of a state firm. The management board is responsible for business decisions. The Assembly of Workers plays the role of executive body. The functions of the Assembly of Workers are: codetermination with respect to rewards, employment, planning goals and influencing the decisions of the executive board through their representatives. The assembly also plays the role of the unions, which work through five commissions: health, security, employment, education, cultural and economic and financial. Each commission has the same number of workers: 1/2 are appointed by the Assembly of Workers and 1/2 by the general manager.

Figure 3.1: Organizational Chart of the Management Bodies in the Industrial Enterprises in Algeria

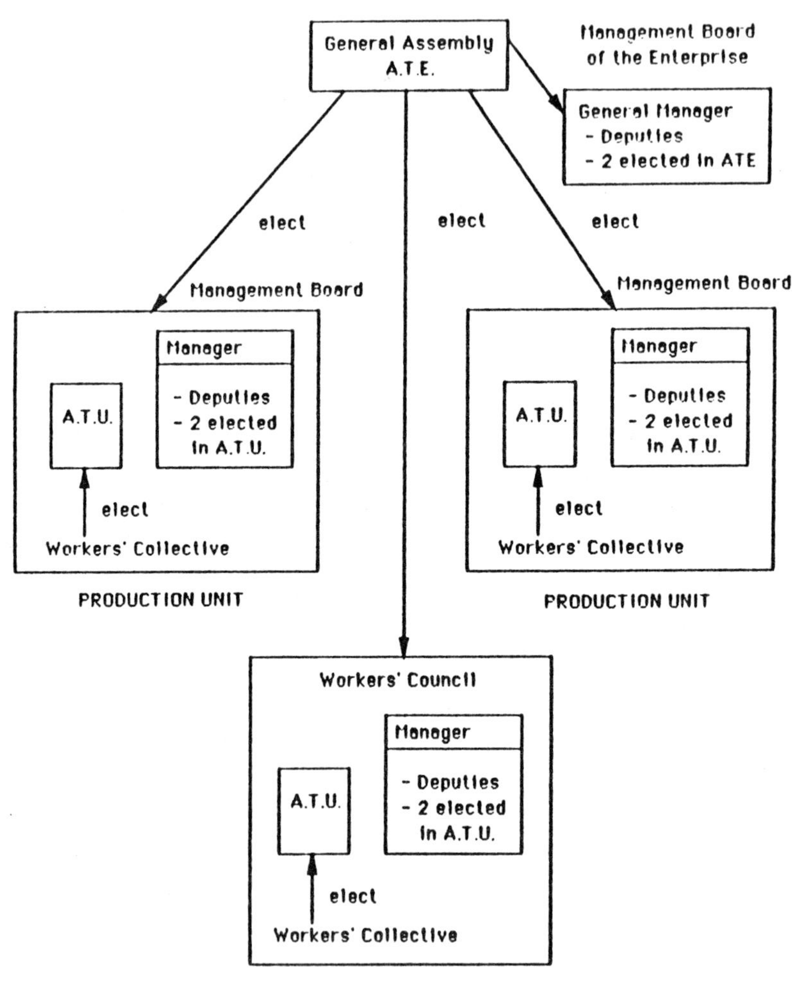

Bangladesh

In firms with over fifty employees, the law allows the existence of workers' committees, consisting of an equal number of workers and managers. They deal with questions of control over the workplace and the distribution of incomes and therefore, their activity is very limited. They primarily discuss questions regarding workers' welfare, productivity and industrial peace. This includes cooperation, mutual trust, working discipline, security and health, improvement of production and other questions regarding welfare.

Bolivia

Figure 3.2 shows workers' self-management in COMIBOL, the Bolivian mining firm. COMIBOL has a tripartite management structure.

Figure 3.2: Organizational Structure of the Management in COMIBOL

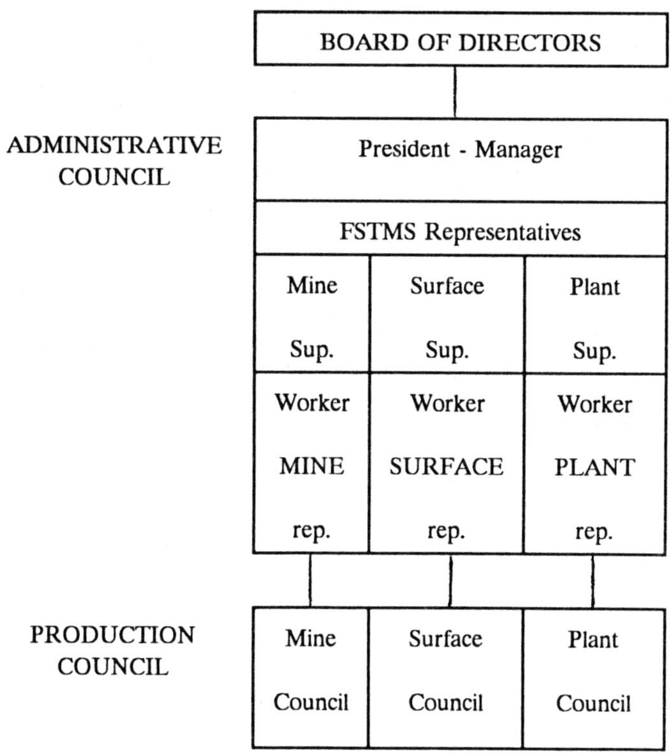

1. Consisting of three workers and three government representatives, the Board of Directors makes business policies for the firm. The leader of the board is a state representative; the next in charge is a member of the union.
2. The Administrative Council is the agency which directs each firm in COMIBOL. It consists of three controllers of production units and three workers' representatives. One member is elected by the union.
3. The Production Council is comprised of six workers which are directly elected. Three of them are then selected to represent workers in the Administrative Council.

Costa Rica

The forms of self-management in Costa Rica are based on a cooperative movement. Figure 3.3, shows that the most important role is played by the General Assembly, which is comprised of members of the cooperative. In order to be a part of the assembly, members must have been working for the cooperative for a minimum of three months and request membership. The General Assembly elects the Administrative Council, the manager, the supervisory committee and the educational committee. The president of the General Assembly is also the president of the Administrative Council, which is the main decision-making body. The General Assembly consists of seven members, five of whom are permanent. The supervisory committee oversees the fulfillment of the directives of the General Assembly. The educational commission organizes training programs for the members. The production committee serves as the liaison between the Administrative Council and all of the members of the cooperative. It determines the tasks of each member in the production process. The Institute for Cooperatives (INFOCOOP) can intervene in the cooperatives if necessary. Moreover, it can impose its policies over those of the General

Figure 3.3: Organizational Structure of the Productive Cooperative in Costa Rica

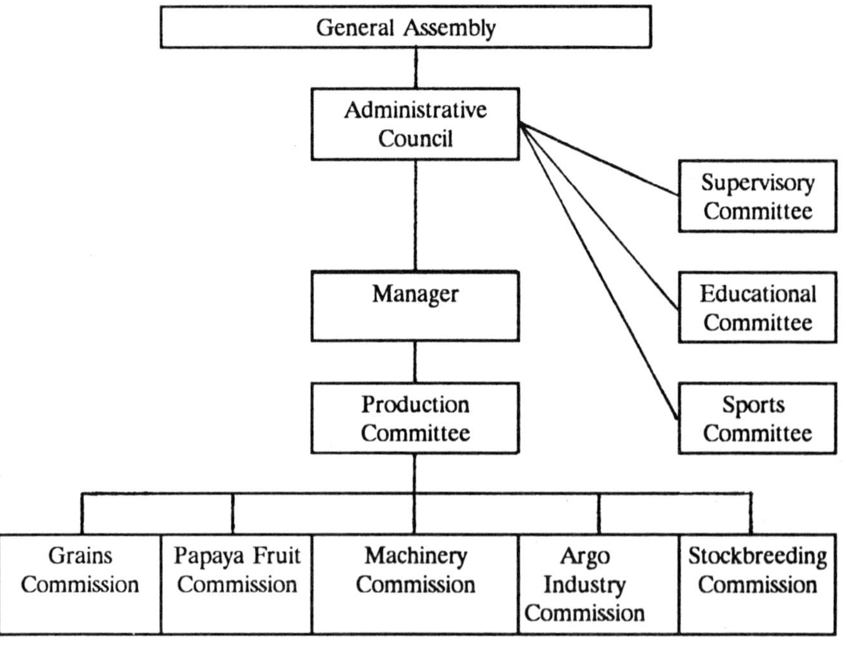

Assembly. It is governed by the Administrative Council and is composed of four delegates from production cooperatives, four members from other cooperatives and three representatives from the government. The institute also defines the working rules of the cooperative (for example, the distribution scheme).

Guyana

In Guyana, workers participate in decision making on three levels. The first level of participation is the Workers' Council, which intervenes in the work units. It consists of management and workers' representatives. The leader is elected by members for a one-year period. The Workers' Council, however, has only a consulting function, and does not handle the problems which relate to the agreement between management and the union representatives, such as wages and employment. Figure 3.4 shows that workers' representatives participate in the Divisional Council. This body does not deal with important problems, but primarily makes decisions involving education, the welfare of workers, job security and cultural and recreational activities. Workers in this division elect one member to represent them on the Board of Directors.

Representing 15% of all economic activity, the private sector comprises various consulting bodies, also made up of workers, such as Workers-Management Participation Board and Industrial Relations Board. Neither in the public nor in the private sphere do these consulting bodies play an important role.

India

In the past, India attempted to implement different forms of participation. Industrial Disputes Act (1947) introduced Workers' Committees in all firms with over 100 employees. This was a two-tier system in which workers and management discussed the problems concerning working conditions. In 1958, the government introduced Joint Management Councils to serve as a place for workers and management to meet and discuss ways to increase productivity. These councils were fully unsuccessful in fulfilling this task.[1] In 1971, some of the firms experimented with electing workers to the Board of Directors. These attempts also proved to be futile. In 1975 a scheme of Joint Bodies (Joint Plant Council and Shop Council) was introduced. Workers and management discussed the fulfillment of monthly production plans, ways to increase efficiency and job security in Shop Councils. Optimal ways of producing and providing good training were discussed in Joint Plant Councils. Both cases, only involved consultation between workers and management, which did not have an impact on collective agreements between union representatives and the representatives of the owners of capital and the government.

Figure 3.4: Structure in Management in Guyana

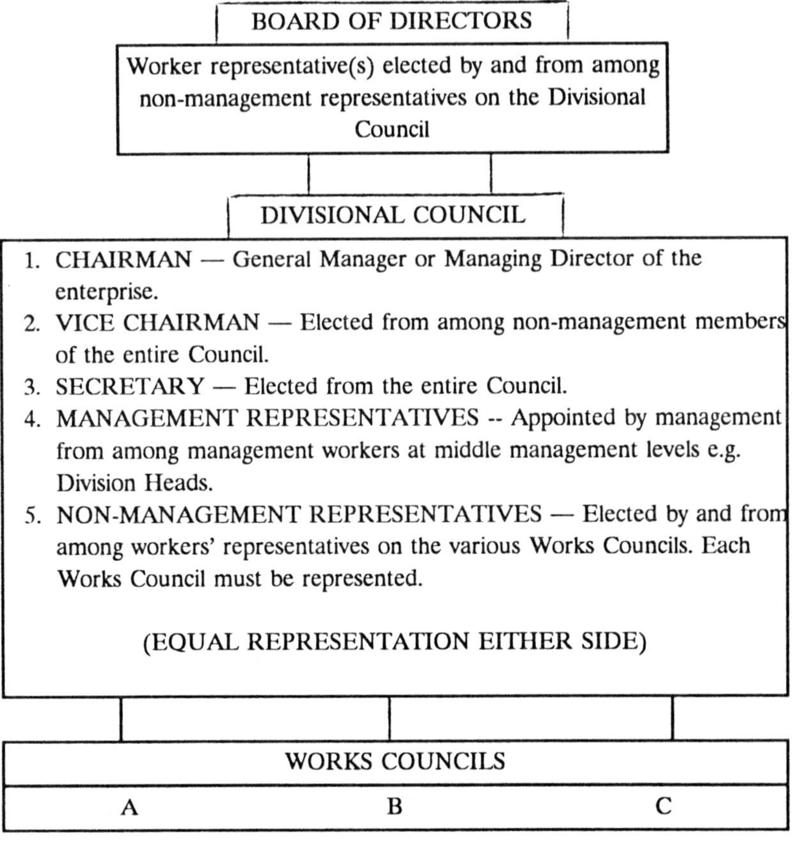

BOARD OF DIRECTORS
Worker representative(s) elected by and from among non-management representatives on the Divisional Council
DIVISIONAL COUNCIL
1. CHAIRMAN — General Manager or Managing Director of the enterprise.
2. VICE CHAIRMAN — Elected from among non-management members of the entire Council.
3. SECRETARY — Elected from the entire Council.
4. MANAGEMENT REPRESENTATIVES -- Appointed by management from among management workers at middle management levels e.g. Division Heads.
5. NON-MANAGEMENT REPRESENTATIVES — Elected by and from among workers' representatives on the various Works Councils. Each Works Council must be represented.
(EQUAL REPRESENTATION EITHER SIDE)
WORKS COUNCILS
A
B
C

Malta

In the Malta Drydocks, participation and self-management is in constant flux. In 1950, the Port Workers Ordinance was introduced in which workers decided to manage and cooperate within the enterprise while sharing the fruits of production. In 1965, the government established the Joint Consultative Committee, from which the workers, withdrew in 1967 because they felt ignored. The union (GWU) and The Labour Party of Malta (MLP) required that workers and government representatives manage the firm, with an equal number of workers and government representatives on this committee. In 1975, the parliament accepted the Drydocks Act, which introduced a new form of workers' participation. The enterprise would be governed by a council

Figure 3.5: Workers' Managers, Shop Councils and Joint Councils in India

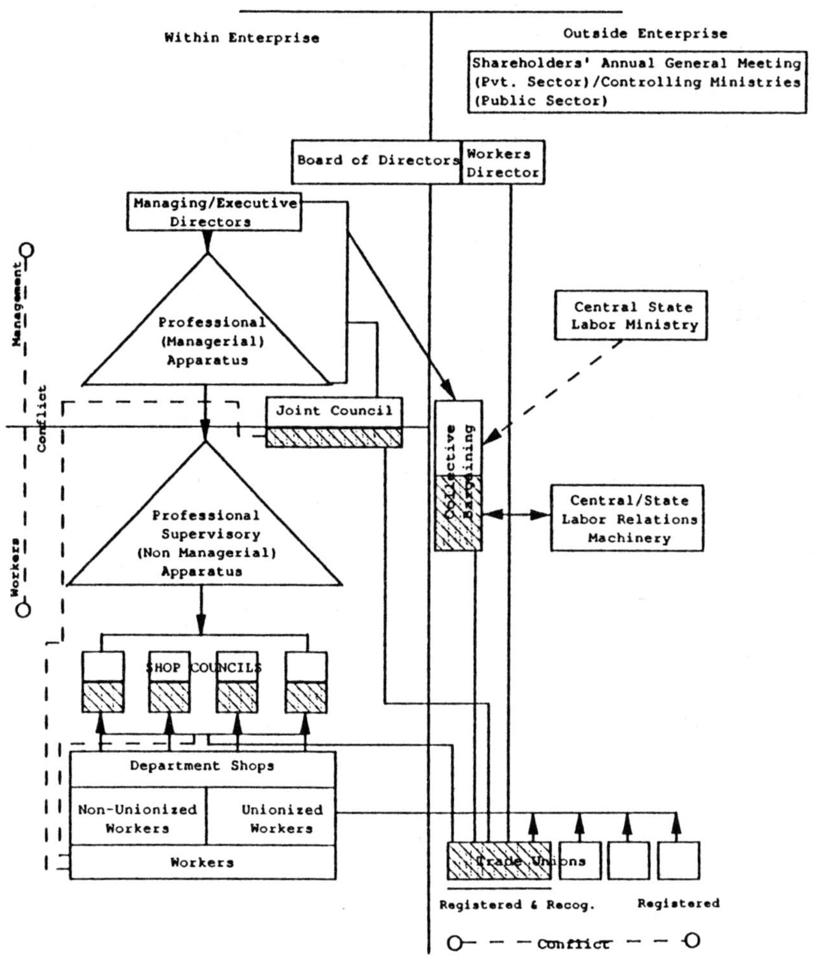

consisting of nine members, eight of whom would be elected by workers. Each candidate would need to obtain at least 100 votes from the general membership. The council would deal with all commercial activities and receive help from committees of five elected members. A leader from management would also sit on the council.[2] Workers' participation was later introduced in all sectors. Workers' Committees which consisted of workers' representatives and management were established. The committee was governed by a manager who was also a manager of a sector. In 1981, the Labour Party of Malta won the elections, giving rise to greater power for the workers' committees and other forms of workers' participation. The present form of organization of workers' participation and self-management is presented in Figure 3.6.

Workers' committees make decisions for the entire sector in conjunction with management. Middle level management establishes similar committees which are composed of members of workers' committees, executive management and union representatives.

Figure 3.6: Self-Management Bodies in Malta Drydocks

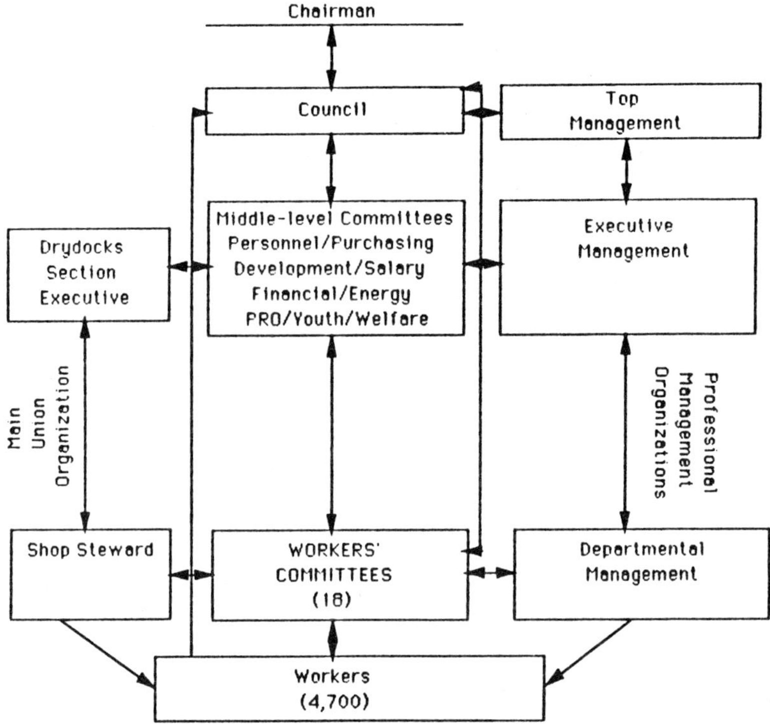

In cooperation with the Drydocks Council and top management, they are responsible for top level decision-making. They handle personnel, sales, purchasing, development and finance questions. They cooperate with branches of workers' committees. This scheme, which was accepted by Malta Drydocks, allows workers to participate in decision-making on all three levels of the decision-making process. This is a type of codetermination as responsibilities of the workers, workers' representatives, management and union representatives are not clearly defined.

Mexico

Management in Mexican cooperatives is defined by the General Law of Cooperative Societies which was enacted in 1939. Figure 3.7 shows that the General Assembly is the most influential administrative body.

The General Assembly meets once a year. Prepared by the administrative council, its agenda consists of voting in new members, changing constitutional acts and electing the administrative board. The Administrative Council is an executive body which is governed by a manager who is elected for a two-year term and can be re-elected only once. The general manager who is responsible for carrying out the decisions of the administrative board is not bound by any term-in-office restriction. Nonetheless, he

Figure 3.7: Organizational Chart of the Management Bodies in the Productive Cooperatives in Mexico

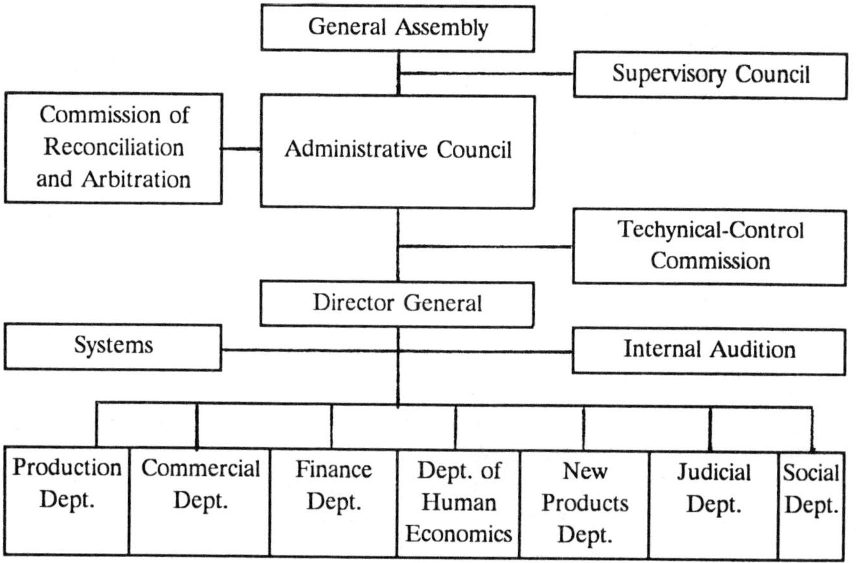

must be approved by the General Assembly. In addition, a supervisory council oversees the activities of the administrative council and the manager, while checking the financial status of the enterprise before the meeting of the General Assembly and various other committees such as the technical committee, the committee for reconciliation and arbitration.

Peru

Participation and self-management of workers in Peru exists in three forms: self-management in agricultural cooperatives; co-determination in labor communities in the industrial sector; and self-management in the social sector.

In agriculture, the government plays an important role in the organization of these cooperatives.[3] In the past the state subscribed to the establishment of production cooperatives and cooperation in management.[4] However, when the government abandoned the management of cooperatives, a new form of management developed. Nowadays, the General Assembly is the top executive body, comprised of members of cooperatives. Its functions include electing members to other committees, checking financial records, determining the distributional scheme and deciding on ways to develop the cooperative. Meanwhile, the Administrative Council actually serves most of the business functions. It consists of five or more members who are elected by the General Assembly. The business is controlled by the Arbitration Council which reports to the General Assembly.[5] There are also special committees which serve as an administrative board. In the management of production cooperatives, there are rules which can be found elsewhere.[6]

Sanctioned by law, the Labor Communities, introduced in "basic" industry,[7] such as mining, fishing and telecommunications. All workers take part in the Labor Community, have a say in the income distribution of the enterprise,[8] and have the right to govern the firm.[9] The Labor Community is managed by the General Assembly, and its executive board is called The Commune Council. The Labor Communities of each particular industrial sector are a part of a larger network. A common fund which is derived from profits and not distributed directly to the workers of the enterprise is distributed to all members of the sector according to work done. In this way, members of each sector share equally in the collective benefits of production, and are not subject to the particular success of an individual firm.

In the social sector, workers govern the firm as it is considered social property. But because the legal owner is not clearly defined,[10] the regional units and the National Assembly adopted some of the managerial functions such as decision- making about the firm's plans and programs as well as its development. Members of the firm can be permanently or temporarily employed. All members of the firm are represented in the Assembly of Workers, which is the highest executive body. The Executive Committee governs the firm, while its members are elected and dismissed by the assembly. Its will and that of the Assembly of Workers is executed by management, which is supervised by the general manager. Workers in the social sector are also members of special committees which were established for the purpose of involving workers in the execution of some tasks ordered by the General Assembly.

Sri Lanka

The law to establish Workers' Councils, which were to to be elected by the workers, was passed in Sri Lanka in 1970. The Councils' task was to provide for the efficient operation of the enterprise by improving productivity and working conditions, as well as by controlling absenteeism. The Workers' Council did not handle questions relating to the working of unions. The results were not promising. Workers did not trust management. Meanwhile, members of the Workers' Council exploited their position by promoting the interests of their political party. This led to management's refusal to cooperate with them and to the unions' fear that the workers' council would usurp all power relations with capital. The new government, which came to power in 1977, abolished all existing bodies of management and replaced them with new Employees' Councils which were to handle primarily questions of industrial peace, productivity, working conditions, and discipline.

The position of the Employees' Council is shown in Figure 3.8. The Council is composed of workers, who are elected for a long term. All other workers participate in the Employees' Council temporarily, according to the needs of the firm. The most important decisions were actually made by the bodies on which workers have no representatives.

Figure 3.8: The Structure of the Management Bodies in the Public Enterprises in Sri Lanka

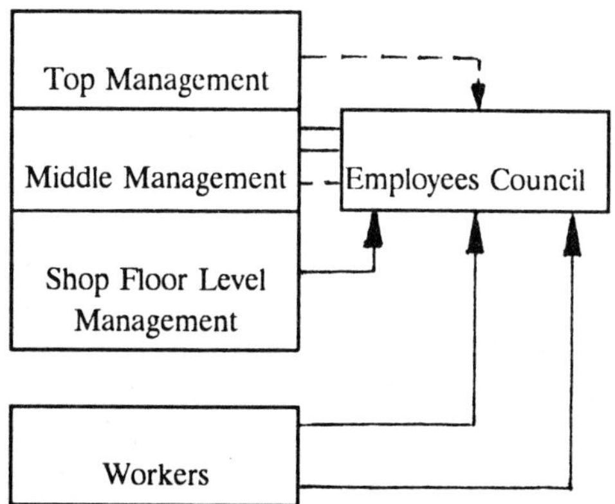

______ Involvement with Employees' Councils on a continuous basis

\- - - - Involvement with Employees' Councils on a non-continuous basis

Tanzania

In Tanzania, participation takes place in both the agricultural and industrial sectors of the economy. In the former, participation in village communes is common place. Besides the economic reasons, political motivation exists for establishing these communes. The commune is managed by the Village Assembly, which is the top management board, and by the Village Council, which is its executive board. However, a member of the Village Assembly is not necessarily a member of the cooperative which executes economic functions, such as production and marketing.[11]

Figure 3.9 shows the executive committee of industrial firms. The first body of management is the Workers' Council which operates in public firms with more than ten workers. Seventy-five per-cent of the members of Workers' Councils are workers themselves while 25% are party members and managers. Members of the Workers' Council discuss questions concerning wages and the government policy relating to them, as well as issues relating to quality of production, planning methods, productivity and income statements. The Executive Committee executes the orders of the Workers' Council and advises the general manager and the board of directors. It consists primarily of experts who evaluate financial and production reports and advise on business policy. At least one member of the Board of Directors is a representative of the workers and is chosen by the union. The General Manager is chosen by the President; the members of the board by the ministry. In private firms, some degree of workers' participation was introduced with the help of the political party in power, some members of which were working in these firms. Their task was to revive the party's influence in the firm and guarantee job security for the workers. In all other instances, firms with more than ten workers had labor committees which were linked to the union organization (NUTA). After 1977, the labor committees associated themselves with the party in power because the unions did so.

Yugoslavia

As mentioned above, Yugoslavia underwent different phases of development of a socialist self-managed society, which can be roughly divided into three phases. The first phase, 1951-1960, is characterized by the introduction of self-management firms, especially in the field of industrial production. The second phase, 1961-1970, described as market socialism in which emphasis was placed on the independence of economic units. The last phase 1971-1988, known as integral self-management, the Basic Organization of Associated Labor (BOAL) has become the main self-management unit and an integral part of the entire structure of the self-managed society.[12] Due to the broad crisis in the Yugoslav economic structure of the last period, Yugoslav society now faces many alternative views on ways to regain economic strength.[13]

Figure 3.9: Management Bodies in Industrial Enterprises in Tanzania

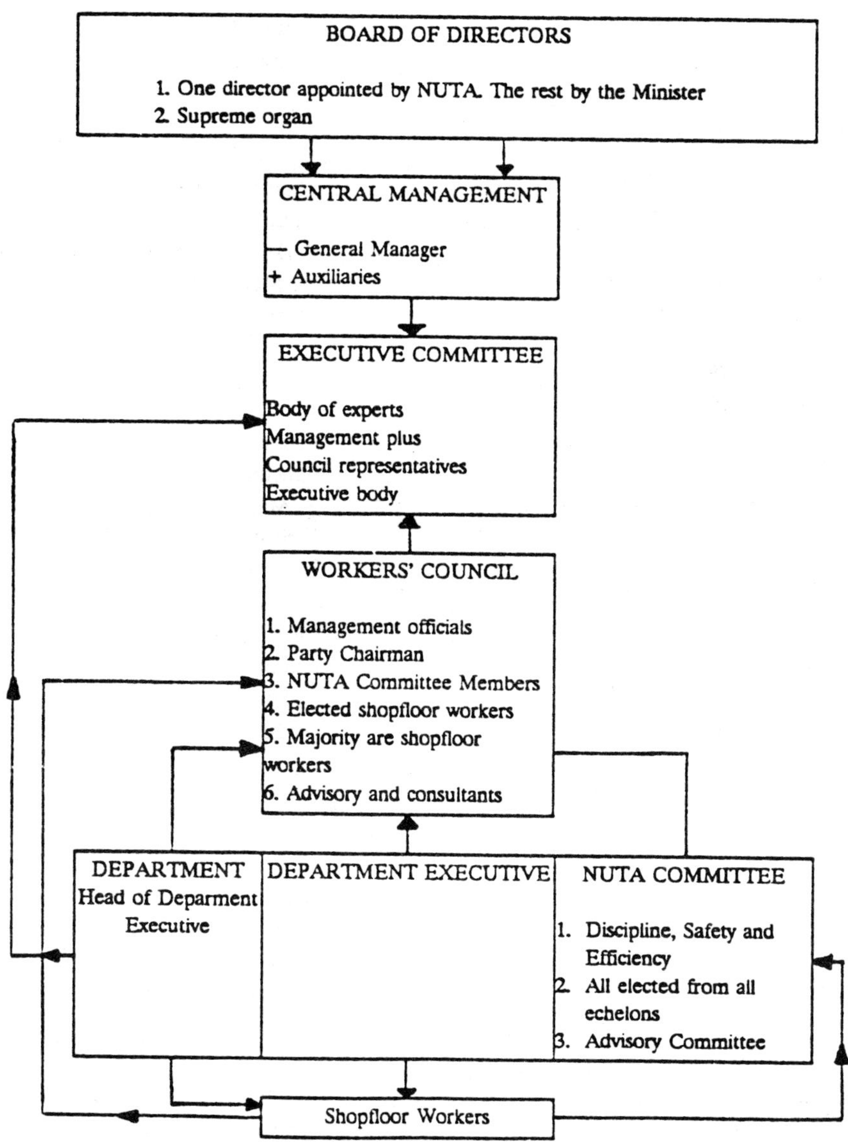

Figure 3.10: The Structure of Management in the Yugoslav Self-Managed Enterprise

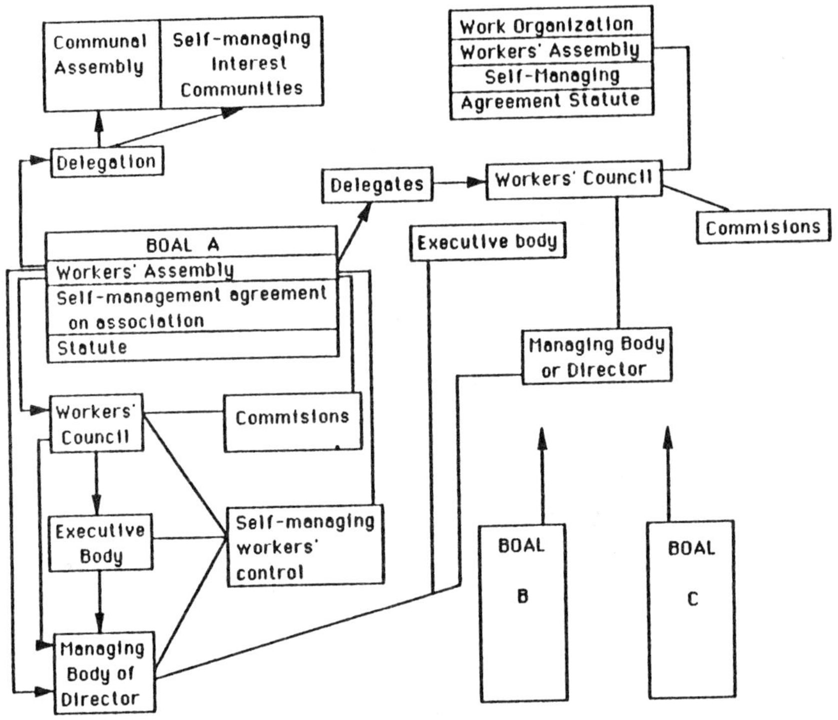

These alternative views are the result of changes in the system of directing and managing firm which was established in the Constitution of 1974, as well as by the changes in the Law of Associated Labor in 1976.[14] But in reality, substantial modifications of the management of socially-owned enterprises have not yet been attained. Figure 3.10 presents the structure of self-managed decision making in working organizations which are composed of BOALs.

Workers' decision-making in BOALs is based on either face-to-face communication or a system of delegates. Questions which affect the essential interests of workers in each of the BOALs, such as self-management agreements on the association of workers in BOALs, changes in the form of organization, bylaws, or basic plans, engender decision-making in the form of referenda and workers' assembly. The questions related to the joint interests between BOALs and the whole working organization, or higher forms of association, are addressed by delegates. The workers' councils within the BOALs consist of delegates from all parts of the working organization. The most important legal obligations of the workers' council are:

1. Preparing bylaws and giving directives to the plans of the BOAL;
2. Deciding on the appropriate business policy and taking the necessary precautions;
3. Approving the plan of the BOAL; and,
4. Approving periodical and final balance sheets.

The workers' council works in conjunction with other committees, such as those concerning employment and labor relations.

Zambia

The legal basis for the introduction of workers' management in public firms in Zambia was sanctioned by The Industrial Relations Act in 1974, but, in practice, was implemented in 1976. The law requires that the workers' councils must be introduced in all public firms with over 100 workers. The law also requires that one-third of the workers' council consist of management and that two-thirds consist of elected workers. Workers have the following legal rights:

1. To be informed of all decisions made by the board of directors or management, including those about investment policy, finance, profit distribution, planning, wage policies and the election of important managerial personnel;
2. To be consulted on issues of social welfare which affect them, such as health and job security; and,
3. To be be informed of the hiring and firing of labor relations personnel. The council can veto decisions concerning the hiring of workers, their wages, their transfer, and their discipline.

Notes

1. The most important reasons for this are the lack of trust between workers and management.
2. In 1977 the Labour Party of Malta introduced the Management Committees in eighteen firms.
3. The state upholds that each member invest in a share of the cooperative. On this basis, the cooperative issues stock, which can neither be sold on the capital market nor have a higher value than its nominal one. In this way, the Paid Corporate Fund is formed to guarantee that the cooperative consist only of its members and not hire employees.

4. A special committee handles sales, personnel, accounting, and deals with questions of liquidation and bankruptcy.
5. The General Assembly decides on how to distribute profits according to the following criteria: (a) limited interests on invested sources of members (not more than 6%); (b) distribution of profit into various funds: 45% to 75% of profits go into the reserve fund, the investment fund for the development of the commune system, the education fund and the fund for cultural and recreational purposes; and, (c) the residual of the profits are divided among the workers according to work done.
6. In some sense the structure of production cooperatives and their governance is similar to that of the Mondragon system.
7. "Basic" industry refers to steel, other metals, chemical, fertilizer, concrete and paper industries, all of which were nationalized by the government.
8. Only 15% of annual profits can be distributed to the Labor Community, which then uses the money to reinvest or purchase shares from the owners of capital who do not work in the firm. The capital, which belongs to the Labor Community, cannot exceed 50% of the firm's capital. If its share becomes larger than 50%, the excess must be distributed to workers according to seniority. This model was modified in 1977. Only 13.5% of annual profit was distributed to the workers in the form of workers' shares while nothing was distributed to the Labor Community. The shares received by the workers can be distributed in various forms: (a)workers' shares; (b) workers' bonds, which are issued by the firm; (c) workers' bonds, which are issued by The Industrial Bank of Peru and (d) Certificates of Social Purposes, which are issued by the firm. The first form represents the net present value of the firm. Workers' bonds are actually loans and therefore do not represent the value of the firm. They merely reflect the short- and long-term liability structure of the firm. Certificates of Social Purposes are issued in order to pay for education, housing, etc. Dividing capital between the workers did not permit the formation of the General Assembly of shareholders. Workers were always a part of the decision making process through their representatives on the executive board.
9. The executive board of the firm must have at least one representative from the Labor Community. The number of managers, who are elected from and by the workers, is increasing due to the increased equity in the hands of the workers.
10. In the classical concept of ownership, there is a clear distinction between the legal owner and the user of capital. In the concept of social ownership, it is not clear who is the legal owner and who is merely the user of the capital.
11. See Putterman (1984) for a good description of the difficulties of managing village communes in Tanzania. This deals with the problems of the coercion of farmers into communes. This is similar to the problems of the collectivization of farms in Eastern European countries.
12. See, J. Prasnikar, V. Prasnikar (1986)
13. The new legislation made an attempt to transform the system of "associated labor" into mixed- ownership economy. In this system, workers self-management would not be the exclusive element in decision-making in Yugoslav enterprise, but in many case would be supplemented by some kind of codetermination.

14. The Constitutional Amendment in 1989 and the Law of Enterprises in 1989 changed the existing legal environment by introducing different types of enterprises. At the same time, the socially-owned enterprises changed their internal structure to one similar to the internal structure of joint corporations. However, at this time, it is still to early to judge what will be the result of such changes.

4

Practice of Participation and Self-Management in the Developing Countries Under Study

Until now, the forms and institutions of participation and self-management, and its proponents and phases of development in certain developing countries have been analyzed. On the basis of the above findings, the countries have been classified into four groups. The first group consists of Algeria, Peru, Tanzania and Yugoslavia, countries which attempted to institute self-management and participation on a national level. The second group is comprised of Bolivia, Costa Rica, Malta and Mexico, those countries which developed participation and self-management only in selected areas. The third group represents India, Sri Lanka and Zambia which developed participation and self-management in the framework of the philosophy of industrial peace. The fourth group includes Bangladesh and Guyana, which developed only elementary forms of participation.

When discussing the operation and results of participation and self-management in these countries, it is reasonable to distinguish the first group from the second. Moreover, enormous differences among the four groups of countries in the way they introduce and promote workers' participation and self-management prevent the study of the impact of workers' participation and self-management on a larger scale. It is impossible to isolate the factors connected to the introduction of participation and self-management and measure the extent to which it influenced socioeconomic development in these countries. Thus, the international comparison of the efficiency of these countries cannot be used in determining the relative success or failure of participation and self-management. However, case studies of the countries in question which were prepared for this study can be compared. This will uncover ways in which participation and self-management function, and to what degree it affects the economic efficiency and welfare of workers. To this end, the basic characteristics of firms in various countries and the formal degree of development of participation and self-management permitted by their institutional structures will first be presented. The formal degree of participation and self-management will be compared to that which actually exists in each of the firms. Next, the economic possibilities of participatory and self-managed firms under study will be presented, taking into account the problems mentioned in the beginning chapters and examining the degree of welfare that they generate.

Basic Characteristics of Firms and the Degree of Formal Participation

The firms studied can be characterized by: the manner in which they were established; their formal structure; their form of ownership; their importance in the economy; their economic activity; and, the possibility of introducing workers in their management. In Table 4.1, the first, fourth, fifth and sixth characteristics are compared.

If one follows Pryor's specifications[1] on the motives for establishing participatory production forms, such as production cooperatives described above, one must indicate that in the selected firms, all five reasons for establishing cooperatives are found:

1. To provide equal rights to all in decision-making (and thus reduce alienation) and guarantee the economic freedom of firms (decentralization). Yugoslav firms such as Alumina, Brewery Union and Industry of Motors Rakovica are the best examples of this;
2. To provide employment and economic development in depressed areas. Coope-Silencio in Costa Rica is an example of an agricultural cooperative established by people without land or employment with the aim of restoring the normal socioeconomic and cultural conditions for living;
3. To fulfill the larger interests of the society and implement some degree of participation and self-management. Many firms in the sample were established by the government with this intent while industries were nationalized;[2]
4. To reap the benefits of mass production and economies of scale. These cooperatives are typically based on the use of modern technology and the requirement for cooperative ownership. The Deeder Cooperative Society in Bangladesh and Koleparke in Peru are examples; and,
5. To permit workers to buy a firm in bankruptcy. Cruz Azul in Mexico is an example. The Contex metal cooperative in Peru was developed with more complicated goals in mind.[3]

Setting aside the Greemen Bank Project in Bangladesh for a moment, which is a special organizational form of guaranteeing financial support for poor people without land, the selected firms can be put into three groups: state and public firms; workers' cooperatives; and, self-management firms of the Yugoslav type. Because of this, the findings cannot be generalized. However, the particular group to which a firm belongs as well as the individual nature of the firm itself will always be considered.

It is possible to divide the ways of establishing participatory and self-management production units in the following manner.

1. Develop from existing units with nationalization or the association of units with different ownership structures, such as COMIBOL, Malta Drydocks, National Bank of Commerce and ROP Limited. (Workers' participation was introduced in all four cases after changes in the ownership and organizational structure. But this is not only the characteristic of public or state firms, but also of Yugoslav firms like Industry of Motors Rakovica and Brewery Union);
2. To establish from scratch, usually with the technical and financial help of foreign firms or governments; such as Urafiki Textile Mill, BHEL - Heep of Hardware Division and Alumina;
3. To function on the basis of class struggles and the transformation of previous private firms.

Therefore, it is evident that the historical environment can contribute to the formation of particular forms of workers' participation, but the sample of firms is so small that a more detailed classification is not possible.

The firm in the sample contribute in varying degrees to their national economies in terms of their production, employment, taxes, investment and balance sheets. COMIBOL contributes a great deal to the financing of the oil industry and to the infrastructure of Bolivia producing 70% of all mineral in Bolivia.[4] COMIBOL is the firm on which the entire economy is dependent. Bharat Heavy Electricals Limited (BHEL) does not play such an important role in the Indian economy rather, it is essential to the production of electronic gear in India.[5] Employing 5% of all workers Malta Drydocks is a leading enterprise in Malta, and is essential to the operation of the entire economy. Urafiki Textile Mill is the largest employer in Tanzania; regarding employment, investments in fixed assets and valued added, Sri Lanka Ports Authority (SLPA) is one of the most important enterprises in Sri Lanka. It is an example for other enterprises to follow distribution of wages and various forms of collective consumption. Other enterprises which belong to the class of productive cooperatives are Cruz Azul in Mexico and Deeder Cooperative Society in Bangladesh. Of course, the cooperatives cannot play the role of public enterprises in the national economies. However, they are important stimulators of social development within the environment in which they have been developed. In conclusion, Yugoslav enterprises will be examined as organizations which operate on a different scale. While they are not the largest, these firms play important roles in their respective industries. For example, the Industry of Motors Rakovica plays a vital role in the production process, the Brewery Union is important in the technology used and Alumina is important in the rapid development of dislocated units from other region, regardless of the republics' borders.

The sample of selected enterprises is also very interesting from the point of view of economic activity and product mix. Concerning the economic activity with which the

TABLE 4.1
BASIC FEATURES OF THE ENTERPRISES UNDER THE RESEARCH

Enterprise	Country	Production	Property Relations	Genesis of the Enterprise	Participation in the Enterprise	Plants	Employment
COMIBOL	Bolivia	ores and metals (1)	state (nationalized in 1952) (2)	old mines from 19th century	1952: some workers' control, after 1983; participatory management	14 mines, 6 industrial plants	27,111 in 1984
BHEL (3)	India	power plant equipment	public enterprise	1956 HEIL, merged with 3 other units in BHEL in 1974	1969: consultative, 1975: Joint Committee	11 manufac-turing plants	69,800 in 1982 18,820 in 1984
Bhopal Unit (HEIL)	India	power plant equipment (4)	public enterprise				
Hardware Division (HEEP)	India	thermal and hydro sets	public enterprise	1967 (USSR technology)			10,777 in 1984

Malta Drydocks	Malta	shipbuilding and repair	public enterprise	prior British defense base	1965: consultative, from 1977 workers' management		4,819 in 1983
Sri Lanka Ports Authority	Sri Lanka	port facilities (5)	public enterprise	before 1958 private, in 1979 merged with 3 public organizations	1980: consultative participation	3 ports	21,648 in 1983
National Bank of Commerce	Tanzania	banking	public enterprise	established in 1967	from 1973 in advisory function	259 agencies, 111 branches in 1982	no data

(1) mining and production of metals (tin, cooper, silver, zinc, tungset, lead etc.)-
(2) the state nationalized the enterprise with payments to prior private owners under the pressure of foreign institutions
(3) BHEL: Bharat Heavy Electricals Limited: HEIL: Heavy Electricals (India) Limited; HEEP: Heavy Electrical Equipment Plant of the Hardware Division
(4) HEIL: hydro, thermal, nuclear, marine and miscellaneous equipment; HEEP: large thermal sets, turbines, electrical machines, gears, large-size steam turbines and generators
(5) including: cargo handling, navigation, tally and security services, supply of other port facilities

(continues)

Table 4.1 continued

Enterprise	Country	Production	Property Relations	Genesis of the Enterprise	Participation in the Enterprise	Plants	Employment
Urafiki Textile Mill Ltd.	Tanzania	textiles	public enterprise	built in 1968 with Chinese assistance	from 1972 in advisory function	5 units	5,111 in 1983
ROP Limited	Zambia	foods and chemicals (6)	public enterprise	merged in 1975 with 2 public enterprises	1976: as consultative body		1,362 in 1984
SONACOB	Algeria	trade and services (7)	state enterprise	1970 from professional group BOIMEX	codertermination from 1978	head quarters and units (8)	2,027 workers
Cruz Azul	Mexico	cement industry	cooperative	founded in 1881, 1931-1934 struggle for the cooperatative	self-management	2 plants, general office	1,396 in 1983, 885 members

Coope-Silencio	Costa Rica	agriculture (9)	cooperative (10)	established in 1973	self-management	2 plants, general office	328 members from 68 families in 1983
Deeder Cooperative Society	Bangladesh	banking, business, insurance	cooperative	1960, a meeting of 9 founders	self-management		1,110 members in 1983
Grameen Bank	Bangladesh	banking	cooperative	no data	no data	no data	no data
Contex	Peru	metal-manufacturing industry	cooperative	no data	workers buy-out	no data	no data
Kolkeparke	Peru	agriculture	social	no data	no data	no data	no data

(6) product mix: edible vegetable oil, fats, soaps and non-soap detergents, toothpaste, shampoos, scouring powders and kitchen detergents, stockfeed cakes

(7) state monopoly over the export and import of the production of wood products 7.

(8) headquarters and 6 divisions, port, stores and services

(9) crops, rice, maize, papaya fruit, sorghum, fodder, extensive stock breeding for meat production, food production

(10) ITCO bought the land from Bananera Co. and purchased it to the farmers through credit

(continues)

Table 4.1 continued

Enterprise	Country	Production	Property Relations	Genesis of the Enterprise	Participation in the Enterprise	Plants	Employment
Alumina	Yugoslavia	metal-manufacturing industry (11)	social	1954, later changed production	self-management	8 BOALs, 2 work communities (12)	2,128 in 1983
Brewery Union	Yugoslavia	beer, baker, yeast	social	founded 1864, 1947-1950 state, from 1950 self-managed (13)	self-management	5 BOALs, 1 work community	630 in 1983
Industry of motors Rakovica	Yugoslavia	diesel engines, tractors	social	founded in 1927, 1944-50 state, from 1950 self-managed	self-management	9 BOALs, 1 work community	

(11) product mix: aluminum unfinished products, metal construction, interiors
(12) BOAL: Basic organization of associated labor
(13) in the period 1864-1947 the modalities of private ownership were changed from individual ownership to joint stock company

enterprise deals, it is necessary to mention the diversity of the activities of the enterprises. The enterprises are found in various industrial sectors: agriculture (in the form of cooperatives), mining, trade, various services, banks, food industry. The division of production in various industries is also present within the enterprises.

When considering the production structure, product mix, it can be concluded that:

1. Enterprises with limited diversification of activity such as COMIBOL, Urafiki Textile Mill, Malta Drydocks, Brewery Union exist with no major flexibility in the production supply. In some cases, enterprises such as BHEL, were found seeking higher diversification of production is the aim of guaranteeing new markets and a higher usage of capacity; and,
2. Enterprises with a highly diversified production structure. This is especially true for production cooperatives which, apart from production as such, include other economic, social and cultural activities.[6] The cooperatives sometimes even develop new organizational forms to fulfill the needs of the broader commune which are formally independent economic units, but are linked to the basic unit in various ways.[7]

At the end, the organization schemes for workers' participation will be described. In this field it is also possible to discuss three groups of enterprises: state or public enterprises, Yugoslav enterprises; and, production cooperatives. Usually, public or state enterprises formed some kind of consulting or advisory councils to provide workers with information about decision processes and give workers the right to respond to the information and give suggestions. They were usually tied to the central decisions of the state administration, which not only decides about the plans but also controls their fulfillment.[8] Although it is difficult to address these enterprises with workers management, in almost all cases they emphasize the decentralization of management to give workers higher participation in decision-making. The reports from these enterprises show that, except for limitations of a formal nature in real participation of workers in decision-making, the limitations of real involvement of workers in management bodies, which usually reduce the efficiency of workers' participation in decision-making, are also very important.

The search for the organizational forms which would provide for the involvement of workers in the management of the enterprise is one of the basic reasons for continuous organizational changes when considering the Yugoslav enterprises. The case of Brewery Union for example shows that the four organizational changes in the last ten years aimed to provide the most direct workers' decision-making. While this was primarily the intention of external institutions, it appears that in the Yugoslav context, organizational changes were mainly consequences of overwhelming interference of bureaucratic and administrative decisions and not of an internal need of workers to search for the most efficient organizational form. This brought the Yugoslav enterprise close to the public enterprise than to the self-managed enterprise while introducing doubt into the organizational structure of the Yugoslav self-managed firm.

Formally the cooperative units which prevail in our sample of enterprises such as Cruz Azul, Coope Silencio, Deader Cooperative Society, Greemen Bank, Contex have similar organizational structures. As this was already mentioned in the previous chapter, it will not be discussed further.

Real Participation and Self-Management of Workers in Decision-Making in Selected Enterprises

The degree of formal workers' participation and self-management in the particular enterprise of our sample does not entirely define real workers' participation and self-management. There are enterprises where the formal degree of participation and self-management is very high, but where key decisions are made by external decision-making bodies. Furthermore, the real distribution of power between internal decision-making bodies is very unsystematic. Yet, there are enterprises where formal possibilities for real workers' participation and self-management are considerably low, but where the degree of actual participation and self-management of workers is higher than in the previous case. The next section will address the question of the extent to which workers really participate in key decision-making in selected enterprises. The question of which decisions are the responsibility of the participatory or self-management decisions of workers and how their decisions are actually made will also be raised.[9] Furthermore, the role of management structure in decisions and its opinion on participation and self-management of workers will be analyzed. Separately, the unions and their attitude toward participation or self-management of workers will be studied. At the end the opinion of workers about participation and self-management in selected enterprises will be presented. In this way, the role, which participation and self-management play in the selected enterprises and the degree to which they contribute to economic development can be estimated.

Are Workers Really Participating in Adopting Key Decisions in the Selected Enterprises?

This is a different question. This is a very heterogenous group of enterprises in which participation and self-management did not come into life with full force. Therefore it is very hard to find a common denominator by which to judge the degree of real workers' participation and self-management. The abstract definition of the self-managed enterprise will be used as a norm, by which an estimation of the real participation of workers in the selected enterprise will be made.

This section will begin from the standpoint that a self-managed enterprise is an association of workers with different interests and particular goals. The fulfillment of these goals reflects their well-being and welfare. Therefore the assumption is made that the most general goal of the enterprise is the maximization of workers' welfare.

However, workers' welfare depends on the fulfillment of interrelated goals. Formally, the workers' welfare function can be presented as follows:

$$W_W = (G_1, G_2, ...G_N)$$

This signifies that workers' welfare in the self-managed enterprise (W_W) depends on the fulfillment of goals G_1 to $G_{N,}$ which can be defined as follows:

- G_1 is net income per worker which is the basic economic goal of an enterprise;
- G_2 is income for collective consumption of workers;
- G_3 is internal distribution of personal income including: degree of inequality; and, the scale of workers' relative personal incomes by qualification structure by jobs, and by type of work;
- G_4 reflects employment, security of work, working conditions, and working effort;
- G_5 is self-managed democracy.

This finding explains that maximization of net income per worker in a self-managed firm is only one of several goals, although the empirical studies show it to be the most important one.[10] Other important goals include the fulfillment of common needs in and out of the firm, internal distribution of personal income, employment, job security, working conditions, working effort and self-managed democracy.

The next question is related to the firm's achievement of goals which are part of the function of the worker's welfare. Generally one can conclude that the level of achievement of any result is determined by variables which can be influenced by the decision-making groups or individuals inside or outside the firm. Scheme 1 summarizes the general discussion about the relation between decision-making groups, decision-making variables and the welfare function.[11]

The scheme is based on the assumption that the main cause and consequence chain is as follows: various groups of decision-makers inside and outside the firm influence the decision-making variables and thus influence the fulfillment of workers' goals which further influence the workers' welfare. It is important to note that workers of a particular firm cannot decide all variables which lead to the fulfillment of goals since each firm works in its own environment and external forces (i.e. market) have different influences on the behavior of the firm. However, it is the role of self-management to grant internal decision makers the right to decide most of these variables thereby reducing the influence of external decision makers. Thus, the first standard for determining the character of decision-making processes in the selected firms is defined. If the decisions about the selection of production, the combination of production factors, economies of scale, sales, purchases, investments and financing are made beforehand by external decision-makers, this firm is not defined as a self-managed firm, but rather as a public or state firm. If the decisions regarding these variables are primarily made by internal decision-makers, then the necessary condition for the self-managed decision-making of workers are fulfilled.

The next step for finding the nature of decision-making processes and participation of workers in decision-making is to determine the relation between decision-making processes which consider the firm as an unavoidable entity, (such as a centralistic hierarchical type of a firm) and the decision-making processes which represent the autonomy of particular organizational levels of the firm (such as factories or sectors). The theory states that the self-managed firm must entirely coordinate economic activity and bear business risk. However, each level must have enough freedom so that workers can fulfill their self-managed rights.[12]

Scheme 4.1:

The Relation Between Workers' Welfare, Secondary Objectives, Decisive Variables and Decisive Groups

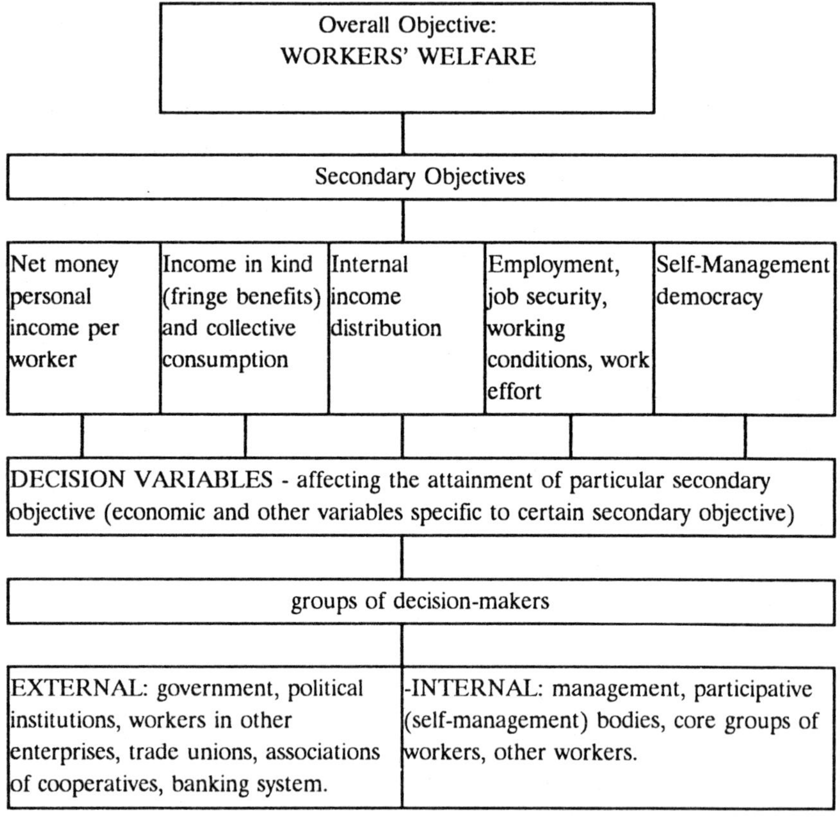

The third criterion in determining self-management decisions of workers concerns the distribution of power among various decision-making individuals within a self-managed firm. According to the model, if decisions are made independently of the

subjective interests and views of any members of the enterprise, this refers to the highest degree of democratic decision-making. Formally, the decision-making process in the self-managed enterprise should be as direct as possible. The decision should be made at the lowest possible level, that is, at the level of the working groups or teams. Because of technical and other reasons such as the size of an enterprise and the importance of the decisions for the entire enterprise, workers also make decisions indirectly through their representatives on the workers' councils and their committees. However, a body which decides about the policy, management is concerned about the interest sphere As such, the leadership concentrates on the coordination of various working tasks and their direction toward the fulfillment of the main goals of an enterprise. These tasks are given to the managerial workers who are also responsible for carrying them out.[13]

If the enterprise meets all three criteria, it is quite independent in decision-making and the external decision-making subjects do not have a major impact on its business and other actions. It also signifies that it has a unified business purpose and that workers directly fulfill their self-managed rights in the working units (functional self-management). A self-managed enterprise is further defined by the degree of intergrity of each individual in the decision-making process as it is evaluated according to the rationality of the decision. Unless these conditions are fulfilled, the firm is not a self-managed enterprise. Rather, it is an other type of enterprise, such as private, public, or state with some degree of participation.

Table 4.2 presents the characteristics of selected enterprises according to the criteria involved. The data reflects that none of the selected firms are fully self-managed enterprises as defined above. With regard to the firms interference of the external subjects in the enterprise decision-making process it is important to stress that all selected enterprises are more or less connected with various state and parastatal institutions. With the exception of the Mexican cooperative, Cruz Azul, all other enterprises from our sample described significant interference in their business by state and parastatal institutions.[14]

With regard to the requirement of autonomy of each level so that the workers can fulfill their self-managed rights, the data shows that the selected enterprises are primarily organized in a hierarchical structure (which is a centralized type of enterprise). In this type of structure major decisions are made in the center; this is especially valid for public enterprises where individual levels do not have major autonomy in decision-making. Exceptions to this are the Yugoslav enterprises, where from the sixties onwards, major efforts have been made to provide business unity through self-managed decision-making of workers in individual work units such as in factories, sectors and plants.[15]

What is the distribution of power in decision-making in the framework of the introduced restrictions between different decision-making groups within the enterprise?

TABLE 4.2
ACTUAL DEGREE OF WORKERS' PARTICIPATION AND SELF-MANAGEMENT IN THE SELECTED ENTERPRISES

ENTERPRISE	COUNTRY	IMPACT OF EXTERNAL GROUPS ON THE MANAGEMENT	DEGREE OF AUTONOMOUS DECISIONS OF THE ENTERPRISE'S DIVISIONS	DISTRIBUTION OF POWER BETWEEN GROUPS IN THE ENTERPRISE
COMIBOL	**BOLIVIA**	The government has a considerable impact on decision-making in COMIBOL. This is determined by the structure of the Board of Directors (1/2 of the members are elected by the government). Problems with sales in the world market require the government assistance.	High degree of centralization of decision-making in the firm.	Operation of the participatory boards is limited. The administrative council is the only working participatory body. Majority of decisions are approved by the Board of Directors.
BHEL	**INDIA**	BHEL operates in conditions similar to all public enterprises. Despite this fact, the Joint	Human Resource Committees are formed in each of the units (Bhopal, HEEP): the executive unit manager, constituted by	The Philosophy of Industrial Peace is the basis of participation. Joint Committees discuss the distribution of profit

unit Bhopal (HEIL) unit HEEP		Committee plays a pivotal role in the relation between management and workers.	sector managers, personnel manager and general manager.	and wages, but have no power. In the participatory bodies management and union leaders dominate.
MALTA DRYDOCKS	MALTA	Because of the crises in the world ship-building industry the presence of the government in decision-making is necessary.	no data	The introduction of participation and self-management resulted in redistribution of power in which workers benefitted. Sixty-eight percent of workers believed that their participation in decision-making increased. Nonetheless, traditional paternalistic views still exist, which reduce the development of participation and self-management. Especially important is the informal power of management in decision-making.

(continues)

Table 4.2 continued

ENTERPRISE	COUNTRY	IMPACT OF EXTERNAL GROUPS ON THE MANAGEMENT	DEGREE OF AUTONOMOUS DECISIONS OF THE ENTERPRISE'S DIVISIONS	DISTRIBUTION OF POWER BETWEEN GROUPS IN THE ENTERPRISE
SRI LANKA PORTS AUTHORITY	SRI LANKA	The state has an important role in decision-making.	no data	Major decisions are made by the boards, on which top management and not workers are represented. The role of the workers' council does not exist in questions regarding to social care. Two reasons for this are: 1) Management's opinion that workers' council is the instrument for the fulfillment of union interests; 2) lack of experience with workers' council.
NATIONAL BANK OF COMMERCE	TANZANIA	The bank is closely related to the government. (Investments in shares are provided by the state.)	Bank's branches are small, without autonomy and coordinated by regional and central boards.	Workers' council has a consultative task which is valid as well for joint workers' council, regional workers' council or industry executive committees.

URAFIKI TEXTILE MILL LTD.	TANZANIA	The government is directly involved in managing this firm. The general manager is elected by the president, while members of the board of directors are elected by the Ministry.	5,000 workers are employed in this factory; there is no decentralization in decision-making.	Workers' council has the consultative role as well as the role in decision-making process.
ROP LTD.	ZAMBIA	ROP is a unit in Industrial Development Corporation (INDECO), entirely owned by the state. INDECO is the main decision-making body, making decisions about investment, finance, sales employment.) The government policy is taken into account.	Centralization of decision-making. In divisional management, the work manager has little freedom in decision- making such as in the purchase of material.	Participation and self-management are not developed. The Law allows consultation between workers and management about questions related to welfare such as food, transportation, housing, medical care, and sports. Workers believe that decisions are made by management.
SONACOB	ALGERIA	The enterprise is involved in the entire planning system of the country. This plan defines its development as well as the ways for its fulfillment.	no data	no data

(continues)

Table 4.2 continued

ENTERPRISE	COUNTRY	IMPACT OF EXTERNAL GROUPS ON THE MANAGEMENT	DEGREE OF AUTONOMOUS DECISIONS OF THE ENTERPRISE'S DIVISIONS	DISTRIBUTION OF POWER BETWEEN GROUPS IN THE ENTERPRISE
CRUZ AZUL	MEXICO	The cooperative was purchased by workers. The external forces are not substantially.	no data	Workers' role in decision-making increased. Workers believe that they participate in decision-making.
COOPE-SILENCIO	COSTA RICA	The cooperative is connected to the government in various ways such as the organization of the business, finance and distribution of income.	no data	The Administrative Council has the power in decision-making. Workers believe that the government will solve all problems.
DEEDER COOPERA-TIVE SOCIETY	BANGLADESH	The cooperative began to operate under the control of the government. Later they separated. External institutions help the cooperative such as in matters of personnel and finance.	no data	The decisions of the government are well- prepared and discussed with the cooperative's members. This is efficient management structure.

GRAMEEN BANK	BANGLADESH	Without external help, Grameen Bank is unable to govern its activity. The bank is hierarchically organized with workers unable influence to decision-making.	The bank functions in 31 units and in 4 regions. Bank employees and project leaders have freedom in decision-making, but are supervised by the central board.	Poor farmers and the unemployed are financed by the bank. Grameen Bank is hierarchically organized and thus, farmers cannot influence decision-making.
CONTEX	PERU	The cooperative was established as a result of the bankruptcy of the private firm. The government's import was high. The government also established a very complicated system of coordination of the cooperatives.	no data	Although the cooperative was established in 1980, Workers' participation is not completely introduced .
KOLEPARKE	PERU	no data	no data	no data
ALUMINA	YUGOSLAVIA	Although there was no industrial tradition, each unit developed rapidly. External decision-making bodies have a great impact in defining business conditions.	Basic organizations which have been dislocated have considerable freedom in decision-making.	Workers' council and self-management boards do not have enough impact in the management of the firm. Experts and management have more power. Forty-four percent of workers believe that the managers have all the power. The information system is not developed.

(continues)

Table 4.2 continued

ENTERPRISE	COUNTRY	IMPACT OF EXTERNAL GROUPS ON THE MANAGEMENT	DEGREE OF AUTONOMOUS DECISIONS OF THE ENTERPRISE'S DIVISIONS	DISTRIBUTION OF POWER BETWEEN GROUPS IN THE ENTERPRISE
BREWERY UNION	YUGOSLAVIA	External groups have a great impact in determining economic conditions such as prices of production resources, distribution of income, investment policy, organization and the decision-making process.	After the changes in the constitution in 1974 the firm was forced to decentralize in BOALS. With a very homogenous production process, this leads to conflicts between BOALS.	Workers believe that power in decision-making is equally distributed in the firm: workers have the most impact on decision-making, than the workers' council, the Board of Directors of a BOAL and finally the Board of Directors of a WO.
INDUSTRY OF MOTORS RAKOVICA	YUGOSLAVIA	The study analyzed the transformation of this firm into a self-managed one. When the firm was state-owned, it was involved in the centralized process of decision-making.	Some of the self-management bodies played no role in decision-making during the period under study.	The manager had all the power during this period. The workers' council had only a consultative role. Discipline and job security were the responsibility of the workers' supervisors.

The reports from the enterprises show that the participation in any of the enterprises is not as developed as was expected.

In public enterprises, important decisions are made in bodies where the workers are not represented, such as the board of directors and top management. The bodies of the workers' participation were either working poorly, as in COMIBOL, or they did not possess the formal power to make key decisions as in BHEL, Sri Lanka Port Authority, National Bank of Commerce, ROP Limited and Sonacob. Only in two public enterprises, the Malta Drydocks and the Urafiki Textile Mill Ltd., was there evidence that workers and their bodies had some kind of impact on decision-making in key business decisions.

Among the cooperatives, there are examples of very successful workers' self-management, as in Cruz Azul and Deeder Cooperative Society. However, there are also examples where the workers did not become considerably involved in decision-making despite formal opportunities for workers' self-management such as in Coope Silencio, Grameen Bank, Contex.

Under these circumstances, Yugoslav enterprises had the most developed formal framework for participation of workers among all other enterprises in the sample.[16] Thus, one would expect real participation of workers in decision-making to be most developed in Yugoslavia. This conclusion is based on reports about the distribution of power in decision-making in the Brewery Union and Alumina. However, these studies reported also some important dissatisfaction. It was directly related to the involvement of workers in the processes of decision-making, as in Alumina, and the tendency for more direct decision-making of workers on the workers' assembly, as in the Brewery Union.

Thus, one can conclude that the model of self-managed decision-making of workers which was developed at the beginning of the chapter cannot be supported by the findings in practice. Workers, who are the source of ultimate decision-making in this model, do not have such power in the decision-making process of the enterprise and thus, none of the enterprises under study can be defined as real self-managed enterprise. To address this question, further investigation into the ways which workers participate in decision making in selected enterprises and of the object of their decision making will continue in the next chapter.

Direct and Indirect Management of Workers in the Selected Enterprises

As organizational forms of worker management in selected enterprises have been discussed above, this chapter will briefly highlight the degree of direct and indirect decision-making of workers in these selected enterprises.

The data in Table 4.3 leads to the conclusion that in public enterprises such as COMIBOL, BHEL, Malta Drydocks, Sri Lanka Ports Authority, National Bank of Commerce, Urafiki Textile Mill Ltd. and ROP Limited, workers participate in decision-making only through their delegates in the representative bodies of workers' management. However, the workers' representative bodies usually have the consulting

TABLE 4.3
DIRECT AND INDIRECT WORKERS' MANAGEMENT

ENTERPRISE	PARTICIPATION OF WORKERS IN MANAGEMENT	SUBJECT OF DECISION MAKING	WORKERS AND THEIR REPRESENTATIVES
COMIBOL	Direct management of workers in the Board of Directors, in the Administrative Council and Production Boards.	Basic strategic and tactical decisions are made by the Board of Directors.	no data
BHEL	Indirect management of workers in the Joint Committee.	Discussions about the questions of welfare such as working conditions, food and income. There are less economic questions.	The relation between workers and their representatives are not suitable. The workers warn that their representatives do not defend their interests. There is internal and external rivalry between members of various union organizations and they do not share a common language.
MALTA DRYDOCKS	Indirect decisions of workers in working committees on questions concerning utilization of capacities, security of work, distribution, welfare and in the Workers Council.	The Board of the enterprise decides the enterprise's strategy, while the committees mainly decide about questions of welfare.	no data

SRI LANKA PORTS AUTHORITY	Indirect management of workers in the Workers' Councils which play a minor role.	The Workers' Councils mainly deals with questions of welfare.	no data
NATIONAL BANK OF COMMERCE	The direct management of workers in the Master Worker's Council, in the Regional Advisory Committee and in the Branch Executive Committee.	Consulting related to the labour productivity such as organization of work, technical knowledge and education, consulting in planning and consulting with distribution of income.	There exists the problem of inappropriate education of workers and their lack of interest. Workers do not give higher priority to participation and self-management.
URAFIKI TEXTILE MILL LTD.	Indirect management of workers in the Workers' Council through general manager, party leadership, members of union's committee, leaders of the sectors, representatives of workers in all sectors.	Consulting about the wage policy, about purchases and sales, quality and quantity of products, planning, balance sheets and income statements.	Performance of working representatives is better than in the above mentioned case.

(continues)

Table 4.3 continued

ENTERPRISE	PARTICIPATION OF WORKERS IN MANAGEMENT	SUBJECT OF DECISION MAKING	WORKERS AND THEIR REPRESENTATIVES
ROP LIMITED	Indirect decisions of workers in the Worker's Council (management workers represent 1/3, elected workers represent 2/3). Except the Workers' Committees which participate in bargaining processes (union) and Party Committee which fulfills the party's statement.	Consulting about welfare questions concerning decisions of the Board of Directors, veto is related to the employment of workers.	There exists bad communication between workers and their representatives.
SONACOB	no data	no data	no data
CRUZ AZUL	Direct management of workers in the General Assembly which controls the working of the managerial structure. The indirect management in the Administrative Council.	The decisions of strategic importance such as statute, the system of distribution, the nomination of the Administrative Council should be accepted by a majority of votes in the General Assembly. The indirect decisions which also exist in the work place are made through functional partcipation. The Administrative Council governs the enterprise and delegates tasks to the managers.	The problem of a two-year mandatory requirement of workers in the representative bodies.

COOPE-SILENCIO	Direct management of workers in the General Assembly. Indirect management in the Managing Committee.	Decisions of strategical importance, such as the election of the Administrative Council, managerial workers and supervisory board in the General Assembly. General Assembly decides the basic operative decisions: business policy, election of managerial workers and general conditions for the working of the managerial workers.	no data
DEEDER COOPERA-TIVE SOCIETY	Direct decision-making of workers in the General Assembly. Indirect management in the Administrative Council.	General Assembly decides the development strategy, discusses and elects the members of the council. It manages the cooperative and decides all short-run decisions which are discussed with the Assembly of members.	The general manager Yasin is the essential person of the entire participatory system. He introduced all kinds of stimulations for the involvement of workers in management.

(continues)

Table 4.3 continued

ENTERPRISE	PARTICIPATION OF WORKERS IN MANAGEMENT	SUBJECT OF DECISION MAKING	WORKERS AND THEIR REPRESENTATIVES
GRAMEEN BANK	Direct management of workers in the project groups.	Members of the project team such as farmers who decide about the economic activity of the group, but are totally under the control of the leader of the group.	no data
CONTEX	Direct decision-making of workers in the General Assembly. Indirect management in the Administrative Council.	The General Assembly is the ultimate decision-making body which meets twice a year and when is necessary.	no data
KOLEPARKE	no data	no data	no data
ALUMINA	Direct management of workers in the Workers' Assembly, with referenda and personal decree. Indirect management of workers with delegates in the Workers' Council of BOAL and WO and through committees.	no data	Very small percentage of workers wish to be elected in the Workers Council (30%); workers believe that the Workers' Council does not represent their interests.

BREWERY UNION	The workers decide directly with personal decree on the Workers' Assembly, with referenda, by signing the contracts and other forms of personal decree. Indirect decisions with the delegates in the Workers' Council.	Direct decisions of workers with referenda concerns the associations of workers in BOAL, WO, COAL; and changes in organization and basics of plan. The summary of direct decision of workers on the worker's assembly is defined by the status discussion of the final report. The workers council makes business policy and works towards its fulfillment. Its operational tasks include borrowing, lending, planning and preparing final reports, among other duties.	The workers believe that they have to decide directly through workers' assemblies and referenda. They oppose BOAL's parcelling and believe that their representative does not represent their opinions.
INDUSTRY of MOTORS RAKOVICA	In the period of 1945-1950 the manager played a major role in decision-making in cooperation with the state apparatus. The workers had only a consulting role. With the introduction of self-management, the main decision-making body became the Workers' Council. The Board of Directors led the enterprise and was held accountable by the Workers' Council. The manager was the executive body of the Board of Directors.	With self-management in 1950, the main decision-making body became the Workers' Council which dealt with questions of basic self-managed acts, business, education and welfare. Nowadays, the Worker's Council instructs and controls the Board of Directors.	no data

role, especially in the field of workers' welfare. They have almost no impact on key decisions of the enterprises. The exceptions are in COMIBOL where workers participate on the board of directors and in the Malta Drydocks through workers' council where the workers are involved in the bodies which make the basic strategic business decisions.

The status of some of the cooperative enterprises such as Cruz Azul, Coope Silencio, Deeder Cooperative Society, Grameen Bank and Contex is similar to that of the typical cooperative managerial and organizational structure. The assembly of all members of the cooperative and its elected executive body make key decisions in the enterprise. Cruz Azul and Deeder Cooperative Society are good examples of this. Coope Silencio is still too dependent on the help of the state institutions. By the nature of its activity, Greemen Bank is almost a state institution, but stimulates participation of workers in project groups. The Peruvian metal processing cooperative, Contex, is still fighting with the growing pains of workers' participation and self-management and despite its formal introduction self-management, does not function.

It is important to note that Yugoslav enterprises such as Alumina and the Brewery Union have the most developed forms of direct and indirect decision-making by workers. The study of Industry of Motors Rakovica which described workers' participation in the period of state socialism (1945-1950) reveals its similarity with other enterprises, especially public enterprises. The period is characterized by a management structure in which workers' management had only a consultative job in the Yugoslav enterprises. The studies which were conducted in Alumina and the Brewery Union emphasize the difference between the present and the past, as well as considerable development in the workers involvement in the management of the enterprises. Although the workers of the Brewery Union and Alumina were not content with the nature of their participation in decision-making at the time, in comparison to the majority of other enterprises in the sample, especially to the public enterprises, they enjoyed a higher degree of freedom and participation in decision-making.

Furthermore, one can conclude from the majority of studies that the major problem of workers' participation or self-management in the public enterprises was due to the existence of dysfunctional delegates either on the bodies of workers' representatives or of joint management bodies. BHEL reported that the relations between workers and their representatives were not satisfactory. The workers complained that their representatives in the Joint Committee did not protect their interests. This could be attributed to the internal and external competition between the members of the union's groups. The report from the National Bank of Commerce stated that workers were not sufficiently educated well and that there was a lack of information from the workers' representatives to their constituents. In ROP Limited there was poor communication between workers and their representatives.

Similar problems were also present in the cooperatives and in the Yugoslav enterprises. Cruz Azul reported that the efficient execution of the projected system of self-management of workers was hindered by acts which did not allow the reelection of workers to the representative's bodies. The workers of Alumina criticized their delegates in the workers' council and its committees for not representing their interests and not informing them about their work. Furthermore, workers did not want to be elected to indirect management bodies because they believed that these bodies did not represent their interests. The workers in the Brewery Union had similar opinions and demanded that the right of key decision-making be transferred to the workers' assembly in order to provide the most direct impact on their decision-making.

Thus, the data shows that workers' participation and self-management has succeeded to a limited extent in the selected enterprises. In most of the cases, this is a reflection of formal opportunities for workers' participation. The function of workers' representatives or delegates is often questionable as it is believed that enterprises do not safeguard the workers' interests. Workers in some enterprises are not interested in participating in the management processes. In the entire sample of the enterprises there are only a few, such as Malta Drydocks, Urafiki Textile Mill, Cruz Azul, Deeder Cooperative Society, Brewery Union, where the workers are involved in making key business decisions and in which workers' participation and self-management play an important role in decision-making. Other enterprises were either content with the declared goals or they faced such objective and subjective barriers to the introduction of participation and self-management that they were unable to make any marked progress.

The Role of Management in Decision-Making

Management is the key decision-making body in the majority of public enterprises and its role is defined by the internal laws of the enterprises. Public enterprises are dependent on the execution of a given policy which is executed by the government through appointed managerial workers and the influence of the board of directors. Because of this, it is evident from the given structure of management that the majority of decisions within public enterprises are taken with this framework. Data in Table 4.4 support this assumption.

In production cooperatives, management is carried out on a different basis as managerial workers are given the task of executing the requirements decided by the workers' assembly and its executive body. Apart from this, it often occurs that people who are willing to participate on a cooperative basis become members of the cooperative. The examples of cooperative behavior of managerial workers are more frequent in the cooperatives such as Cruz Azul, Deeder Cooperative Society and Grameen Bank. However, in cooperatives the lack of professional skills of managerial workers is often evident, as seen in Contex. The experiences reveal that the problem is easier to overcome in cases of isolated cooperative movements as in Cruz Azul,[17] where successful managerial workers who will work according to cooperative principles are found within the environment, than cases where cooperatives operate in a competitive environment.

The tasks of managerial workers in the Yugoslav enterprises are defined precisely by the existing laws and appropriate internal bylaws. Formally, managerial workers lead

TABLE 4.4
THE ROLE OF THE MANAGEMENT AND ITS VIEW ON PARTICIPATION AND SELF-MANAGEMENT

FIRM	COUNTRY	THE ROLE OF MANAGEMENT IN DECISION MAKING	MANAGEMENTS OPINIONS ON SELF-MANAGEMENT AND PARTICIPATION
COMIBOL	BOLIVIA	Management and unions are struggling for the achievement of power in decision-making. The management is elected by the government.	Technical personnel and management believe that workers' participation decreases efficient decision-making.
BHEL (3) Bhopal unit (HEIL) HEEP unit	INDIA	Management has all the power in decision-making.	Management is interested in preserving the structure and the role of the joint committees. Management wishes that union leaders and workers' representatives involved in participation.
MALTA DRYDOCKS	MALTA	Management is still the central decision-making body. The introduction of self-management decreased its power, but informally the situation has not changed.	no data
SRI LANKA PORTS AUTHORITY	SRI LANKA	Main decisions are made by the management. The role of the workers' council is limited by laws.	Management negatively evaluates the role of participation and self-management. Conflicts between management and workers resulted in the abolishment of workers' councils.

NATIONAL BANK OF COMMERCE	TANZANIA	Decision-making is exercised by the management. Workers have little freedom in giving advice and influencing decisions.	Management is satisfied with the existing role of workers' involvement.
URAFIKI TEXTILE MILL LTD.	TANZANIA	Chinese experts built the factory. Management is inclined toward socialism and is willing to cooperate with unions.	The management structure supports participation and self-management.
ROP LTD.	ZAMBIA	INDECO advises the general manager, who fulfills the tasks with the help of the workers' committees. Participation is introduced on the basis of the Philosophy of Industrial Peace.	The general manager does not attend the meetings of the Workers' Council. The leading management structure negatively evaluates the role of participation.
SONACOB	ALGERIA	no data	no data
CRUZ AZUL	MEXICO	Management fosters the policy of the General Assembly and the Administrative Council. The general manager is responsible for the coordination of tasks, given by the Administrative Council.	Management is trained in the cooperative spirit.

(continues)

Table 4.4 continued

FIRM	COUNTRY	THE ROLE OF MANAGEMENT IN DECISION MAKING	MANAGEMENTS OPINIONS ON SELF-MANAGEMENT AND PARTICIPATION
COOPE-SILENCIO	COSTA RICA	The Administrative Board has the largest power in decision making. It consists of a president, a vice president, an advisor, two elected members and a manager. The manager represents the enterprise and is responsible for the fulfillment of tasks, which are defined by the Administrative Council.	no data
DEEDER COOPERATIVE SOCIETY	BANGLADESH	An example of an efficient participatory management: (1) disseminating giving information; (2) allowing participation of workers; and, (3) distributing the surplus.	The management structure and especially the general manager support the participation.
GRAMEEN BANK	BANGLADESH	The management and the employees of the bank support the involvement of unemployed workers no new projects on the basis of participatory management.	The management structures and especially general manager support worker participation.

CONTEX	PERU	The general manager is promoted on the basis of competition. A lack of skilled workers to manage the firm.	Main problem is the lack of capable management.
KOLEPARKE	PERU	no data	no data
ALUMINA	YUGOSLAVIA	Despite formal limitations, the management has high informal power in decision-making.	Management evaluates workers' interests as being short-term oriented and therefore as being in contradiction with the growth of the firm.
BREWERY UNION	YUGOSLAVIA	Formally, the task of management is to manage the enterprise, suggest business policy, organize the working process and fulfill the Workers' Council tasks. Management has informal power in decision-making.	Management supports workers' self-management.
INDUSTRY OF MOTORS RAKOVICA	YUGOSLAVIA	no data	no data

the enterprises, propose business policy, coordinate the activities of the workers' council and execute their decisions.[18] From this perspective, the managerial workers cannot make decisions which directly concern the status of any individual or individual groups in the enterprise, In this framework, the following rule is valid: one man-one vote. In spite of this, managerial workers have a major influence on decision-making as the study of the Yugoslav enterprises shows.[19] It particularly emanates especially from their position in decision-making,[20] and is objectively determined by the nature of the decision-making processes. This influence cannot be taken away from the managerial workers, and in Yugoslavia, this results in the following absurd situation: since the influence of managerial workers in the decision-making process is not legally supported, they do not bear the responsibility for their decisions. Both Yugoslav studies regarding Alumina and the Brewery Union warn about such non-coordination, and support the demand for a thorough reformulation of the philosophical suppositions of the Yugoslav self-managed model, which assumes total homogeneity of workers' interests in a particular enterprise.

The conclusion of this chapter is that the power in decision-making which is given to the managerial workers in the selected enterprises is a very important factor in decision-making processes. To some degree it is the result of the institutionalized structure of the management and leadership in the enterprises especially in public enterprises. However, the same tendency can be found in those organizational forms where this influence is not institutionally built into the decision-making system as it is in the cooperatives and in the Yugoslav enterprises. The degree of cooperative behavior of the managerial workers under these conditions therefore determines how the process of decision-making will perform and whether this kind of decision-making will lead to efficient results. Of course, as information, and its use, combined with the speed of the decision-making are so crucial to efficient decision-making, the cooperative behavior of the managerial workers is not a guarantee for the efficiency of these decisions.

The Relation of the Unions to Workers' Participation and Self-Management in the Selected Enterprises

The importance of unions in building participation and self-management in the developing countries was examined in discussions on the origins of participation and self-management. As the data presented in Table 4.5 substantially supports the stated views it will not be discussed further. At this point, important findings about the views of unions toward participation and self-management in the selected enterprises can be derived from the data:

1. Unions generally do not oppose the involvement of workers in the enterprise management. There are important differences among public enterprises,

TABLE 4.5
THE RELATION OF UNIONS TOWARD PARTICIPATION AND SELF-MANAGEMENT

ENTERPRISE	COUNTRY	UNIONS ABOUT SELF-MANAGEMENT OR WORKERS
COMIBOL	BOLIVIA	The relation of a particular leader of the union toward participation and self-management varies and depends on their party's position.
BHEL (3) Bhel (HEIL) Unit HEEP	INDIA	There exists internal and external rivalry between union's representatives. As there is no coordinated action they cannot reach a consensus. Otherwise the unions are more interested in the bargaining procedure.
MALTA DRYDOCKS	MALTA	Ninety-eight percent of industrial workers are involved in the General Workers' Union. The role of unions in the entire process of decision-making is unclear even though they support participation.
SRI LANKA PORTS AUTHORITY	SRI LANKA	Unions are not unified. Majority of workers are involved in the National Workers' Union which is a part of leading party, UNP.
NATIONAL BANK OF COMMERCE	TANZANIA	Workers are involved in the national union (JUWATA) which is a part of the leading party (CCM), which supports the workers participation.
URAFIKI TEXTILE MILL LTD.	TANZANIA	Workers are involved in the national union (JUWATA) which is a part of the leading party (CCM) which supports participation and self-management.

(continues)

Table 4.5 continued

ENTERPRISE	COUNTRY	UNIONS ABOUT SELF-MANAGEMENT OR WORKERS
ROP LTD.	ZAMBIA	The members of the union are organized in the Worker's Committees. They deal primarily with the questions of wages and working conditions. They cooperate with the bodies which deal with worker's participation.
SONACOB	ALGERIA	no data
CRUZ AZUL	MEXICO	The unions in Mexico do not support participation and self-management.
COOPE-SILENCIO	COSTA RICA	no data
DEEDER COOPERATIVE SOCIETY	BANGLADESH	no data
GRAMEEN BANK	BANGLADESH	no data
CONTEX	PERU	The unions support the cooperative organizations that guarantee the employment of workers.
KOLEPARKE	PERU	no data
ALUMINA	YUGOSLAVIA	There is no specific statement about the opinion of the union.
BREWERY UNION	YUGOSLAVIA	The union in the WO supports self-management with the tendency to provide a higher presence of workers in laying the groudnwork for decision-making.

cooperatives and Yugoslav enterprises. The unions' support of participation and self-management in the public enterprises depends on the direction of the most important union organizations within them as in COMIBOL, Malta Drydocks, National Bank of Commerce and Urafiki Textile Mill Ltd. The unions do not have an important role in cooperative units.[21] Because of a unified trade union organization in Yugoslavia, whose program declared the building of a pure and developed self-managed society, it is clear that the union organizations in the enterprises also supported the self-management decisions of workers;[22]

2. In some public enterprises, the militant stance on participation and self-management of several unions is evident. The views of various union organizations about the participation and self-management differ greatly and thus hinder the working of participatory and self-managed bodies. Opposing views therefore, become evident as seen in BHEL, Sri Lanka Ports Authority;
3. Oftentimes a unified union organization in a given country is part of a leading party apparatus, and as such, loses its role in organizing the workers' interests within the enterprise.
4. In the majority of public enterprises it is unclear as to what the role of the unions should be given to the newly established bodies of workers' participation and self-management as in ROP Limited, COMIBOL and BHEL. Workers do not view unions as the protectors of their interests as they do in the Malta Drydocks.

It is therefore possible to conclude that the role of the unions and union organizations in the introduction of participation and self-management is not entirely defined. If the unions completely disappear from the decision-making process, while surrendering their role to the self-management and participatory bodies, workers may lose their legitimate power in decision-making. They will perform as unorganized individuals in decision-making against the organized groups, as managerial workers do. On the other hand if workers are able to freely select among various union organizations, major differences of opinion arise which are related to the competition among their leaders.

The Views of Workers About the Attained Degree of Participation and Self-Management

Table 4.6 presents the data on the views of workers in the selected enterprises about the attained degree of participation and self-management, the development of the workers' participation and self-management in their enterprises over time, and their opinions on further development. Based on the presentations given, the opinion of

TABLE 4.6
OPINIONS OF WORKERS ON PARTICIPATION AND SELF-MANAGEMENT

FIRM	COUNTRY	Opinion of Workers' on Degree of Actual Participation and Self-Management	Opinion of Workers' Participation and Self-Development Over Time	Opinions of Workers on the Development of Participation and Self-Management
COMIBOL	BOLIVIA	Workers believe that bodies of workers' participation do not function. Sixty-two percent of workers are not aware of self-management acts. They believe that self-managed bodies do not have an important impact on the events.	Unions believe that they deal with class struggle and that participation and self-management should continue.	Workers believe that participation and self-management did not lead to drastic change.
BHEL Unit Bhopal (HEIL) Unit HEEP	INDIA	Majority of workers believe that they can freely express their opinions (Bhopal- 60%, HEEP 50%), but primarily union representatives and management participate in discussions on Joint Committees. Members of Joint Committee think that the workers are satisfied with participation, non-members feel the opposite. Workers in Bhopal are more content than they are in HEEP.	no data	Role of Joint Committee improved.

MALTA DRYDOCKS	MALTA	With introduction of participation and self-management, a better understanding of management and workers was fostered along with the improvement of the workplace. Seventy-two percent of workers believe that participation in the board does not accomplish very much.	Fifty-five percent of workers support further development of participation and self-management, 33% only with specific conditions, 63% think that workers' self-management is most suitable for Malta Drydocks.	68% of workers think that the degree of participation increased over time.
SRI LANKA PORTS AUTHORITY	SRI LANKA	Workers believe that Workers' Council does not play a sufficient role; it does not have any role in forming of wages, but has some role in changing work conditions.	Workers feel that they should have a higher impact than they actually do.	Workers believe that Workers' Council did not fulfill their expectations; only 40.5% believe that Workers' Councils are operating successfully.
NATIONAL BANK OF COMMERCE	TANZANIA	The majority of interviewed workers, 86%, believe that participation functions well.	Majority believe that achieved degree of participation is too small and that steps must be taken to reduce the power of management.	Workers believe that introduction of participation does not considerably reduce the power of management.

(continues)

Table 4.6 continued

FIRM	COUNTRY	Opinion of Workers' on Degree of Actual Participation and Self-Management	Opinion of Workers' Participation and Self-Development Over Time	Opinions of Workers on the Development of Participation and Self-Management
URAFIKI TEXTILE MILL LTD.	TANZANIA	Ninety-five percent of interviewed workers believe that the introduction of participation and self-management in their factory was successful.	Workers believe that participatory process must be improved to decrease conflicts, increase joint responsibilities and thus, increase productivity.	It is shown that over time workers, although uneducated, were involved in important discussions about the strategic development of the enterprise.
ROP LTD.	ZAMBIA	Workers are not familiar with the operation of the Workers' Council. The majority of workers are not familiar with fellow members. Workers' committees have a greater role because of their perceived benefits to workers. The workers believe that they should have more power while management should have less.	Workers demand the right to vote for the president of the Workers' Council. It is necessary to clearly define the relationship between the Workers' Council, workers' committee and party committee.	In 1976, Workers' Council introduced; but in reality, no change took place
SONACOB	ALGERIA	no data	no data	no data

CRUZ AZUL	MEXICO	Workers actively participate in the General Assembly, which they regard as the most important decision-making body in their cooperative.	It is important to develop functional participation. Workers thus become more devoted to the cooperative and do not focus exclusively on the short run.	Workers' participation improved over time, especially in the eighties.
COOPE-SILENCIO	COSTA RICA	Workers positively evaluate participation in decision-making, especially regarding questions of their economic benefit in the form of loans, employment and personal income. They recognize the dominant influence of the govenment.	no data	no data
DEEDER COOPERATIVE SOCIETY	BANGLADESH	no data	no data	no data

(continues)

Table 4.6 continued

FIRM	COUNTRY	Opinion of Workers' on Degree of Actual Participation and Self-Management	Opinion of Workers' Participation and Self-Development Over Time	Opinions of Workers on the Development of Participation and Self-Management
GRAMEEN BANK	BANGLADESH	The goal of the bank is to provide jobs for unemployed farmers. The emphasis is on participation of workers to increase trust between members.	Grameen Bank is a hierarchical organization; no data is available on the opinions of workers.	Workers considerably improved their economic and social status as well as their knowledge.
CONTEX	PERU	The information system is not developed. Workers are not satisfied, but they still remain in the firm. Participation is still not introduced.	Workers believe that the system of participation and self-management within the firm should be reorganized. The major internal problem is related to education and training of workers.	Participation did not have a major impact over time.
KOLEPARKE	PERU	no data	no data	no data
ALUMINA	YUGOSLAVIA	78.6% of workers are aware of their formal rights associated with self-management. They believe that the management and experts have the most power in decision-making. Workers perceive a high degree of the democratic expression of ideas.	Workers believe that their position in decision-making should be improved.	Workers believe that due to direct decision-making, their rights in self-management will increase.

BREWERY UNION	YUGOSLAVIA	Workers believe that external groups have too much of an impact on decision-making. They believe that the introduction of BOALs resulted in a parcelling of their interest. Workers also perceive that power in decision-making is democratically distributed with respect to particular tasks.	Workers would like to increase the degree of the homogeneity in the process of decision-making.	Workers believe that self-management operated most effectively in the sixties, when essential decisions regrding investment, business policy and distribution of income, were the responsibility of workers. The formal rights of workers in the seventies were increased but the decision-making process was not affected.
INDUSTY OF MOTORS RAKOVICA	YUGOSLAVIA	The workers had only a consulting role in decision-making between 1945 and 1950.	no data	The Workers' Council replaced management at the end of the fifties.

workers concerning the level of participation and self-management achieved ranges very favorable, as in the Malta Drydocks, Urafiki Textile Mill Ltd., Cruz Azul and Brewery Union to very negative as in COMIBOL, Sri Lanka Ports Authority, ROP Limited and Contex. The workers' remarks regarding the increase of the degree of real participation and self-management in their enterprises are also similar. Some of the enterprises reported important progress, as did Urafiki Textile Mill Ltd., Cruz Azul, Grameen Bank, while some enterprises did not identify any major changes, as did COMIBOL, ROP Limited and Contex. In Yugoslav enterprises, Alumina and Brewery Union reported that the level of workers' self-management was decreasing.

How to ensure the active role of workers in the process of decision-making is a basic question that is fundamental to all enterprises. It is from this base that workers also evaluate the meaning of further development of participation and self-management in their enterprises. The data fails to indicate a clear direction for development to take. The public enterprises are especially limited by institutional rules regarding the involvement of workers in management. The Comibol and Malta Drydocks experience show that with effective class struggle it is possible to overcome these barriers. But this is only a necessary prerequisite for the actual functioning of participation and self-management.

How the workers should be involved in decision-making is the next question. The model "one man-one vote" which is developed in cooperatives and in Yugoslav enterprises is questionable because it assumes a homogeneous group of workers. In this context, the problem of managerial workers has already been mentioned. It is evident for example that in the Yugoslav enterprises the managerial workers, due to their position in the process of preparation of the decisions, informally influence decision-making even though they do not bear the responsibilities.[23]

The production cooperatives, such as Deeder Cooperative Society, Grameen Bank and to some degree, Cruz Azul, also show that insistence on this model of decision-making depends too much on one or a few persons, usually the manager who personally supports the introduction of this principle. Thus, it is reasonable to state that workers' participation can be explained somewhat differently and that individual workers, and members of the cooperative or the self-managed enterprise will not be on the periphery of the decision-making process. It seems that the bargaining model of the enterprise of Miyazaki (1984) or Svejnar (1982a), in which different parties with similar interests jointly determine the policy of the enterprise is more suitable for workers' participation in decision-making than is the traditional self-managed model of the Ward-Domar-Vanek type, which assumes total homogeneity of workers in decision-making. The next chapter will present a more detailed presentation of this thesis.

Fundamental Findings About Economic Behavior of the Selected Enterprises

Because research in the case studies did not follow specific methodology and failed to provide the necessary information, the findings of the economic behavior of the enterprises under study cannot be presented in the standard format.[24] An analysis of the collected data will attempt to address the questions of the economics of a self-managed enterprise which are presented in the second chapter. First, the findings of the case studies on productivity and the efficient use of production factors through improved technology will be summarized. This will be followed by a summary of the research findings on employment, distribution of income and financing. The analysis will conclude with a discussion of the entry of new enterprises.

Productivity and Technology

Reasons for why the higher degree of workers' participation and self-management has a positive effect on the production efficiency of the enterprises were already discussed and will therefore not be developed further. Rather, the discussion at this point will focus on why labor productivity appears to be the most important economic variable in almost all of the enterprises under study. It seems that there are two kinds of phenomena. There are enterprises which target physical productivity as their highest goal, even over profit-making. Some of these enterprises attribute this to a directive assigned by the state and thus define themselves as mere executors of the public will. There are also cooperatives which attribute higher labor productivity to the fulfillment of members needs which are related to various activities and achieved by the members of the cooperative. In both cases, efficiency, which is quantified by rigorous economic measures, is displaced by the goal of physical productivity. On the other side some of the enterprises estimate that there exists a narrow link between productive efficiency of the enterprises and other measures of economic efficiency.[25] Therefore, in their opinion productive efficiency of the enterprises should be given all attention.

However, the real influence of the introduction of participation and self-management on labor productivity varies with each enterprise under the study. The study of BHEL, for example, demonstrates that an increase in labor productivity and production quality resulted from discussions between management and workers in joint commissions regarding this issue. After 1971, when codetermination was introduced and after 1975, when self-management was introduced, productivity in Malta Drydocks increased by 2-3% per year than 1972 to 1981. Also a report on the of productivity of the cooperative Cruz Azul discusses a longer period of growth of labor productivity. In any case, Cruz Azul is an example of a successful enterprise with a higher labor productivity than the average concrete industry in Mexico.

A good example of a successful self-managed enterprise is described in the Brewery Union case study. In the period 1952-1982 beer production increased by 12 times, total assets by 4 times, and the number of employees by 3 times. In comparison to similar breweries in Europe, the Brewery Union performed with above average production. However, there are other studies which fail to confirm these results. The study of the Sri Lanka Ports Authority, National Bank of Commerce, Urafiki Textile Mill, ROP Limited, for example, fails to mention the major changes in labor productivity after the introduction of workers' participation in these enterprises. The reports from COMIBOL show that productivity fell by 2.4% in 1983 and further by 30% in 1984[26] following the introduction of the participation of management in 1983. This also occurred in the Peruvian cooperative Contex. Thus, one cannot draw a final conclusion from the contradictory evidence.

Moreover, the data shows that some of the enterprises faced the serious problem of technology selection. In the sample, two contradicting effects are recognized. On one side, there are enterprises with highly capital-intensive technology. This tendency is especially present in the Yugoslav enterprises.[27] On the other side, there exist enterprises which are not sufficiently capital-intensive. This is related to a firm's limited access to the capital market. Examples of this type of enterprise are COMIBOL, which uses its reserve source to purchase investment goods, Coope Silencio which has no a suitable financial structure to purchase investment goods, and Contex.

A similar problem is the choice of the optimal scale of production. Theoretically, self-managed enterprises should produce in the range of constant returns to scale (Vanek, 1970). However, empirical research on Yugoslav enterprises gives contradictory evidence about the returns to scale. There exists evidence of increased returns to scale,[28] as well as evidence of decreased returns to scale.[29] Data about the inefficient use of capacity such as increasing returns of scale is also evident from other enterprises in the sample, and the studies give the following reasons: inadequate education of workers and underestimation by management[30] which is related to the previous discussions on decision-making processes in the selected enterprises; and, the constant employment of workers which prevents the adjustment of employment to economic cycles.

On the basis of this data, can one conclude that the self-managed and participatory enterprises behave irrationally in selecting the technology and in adjusting the scale of production to market conditions? There is no a tentative answer to this question on the basis of our sample of enterprises. One can conclude only that there are no observable systematic differences between the enterprises under study which reveal the difficulties of selecting technology and production technique and of determining the scale of production.

The next question is how workers from the sample evaluate participation and self-management. The majority of workers which were interviewed believed that participation and self-management were important factors in increasing labor productivity. Because the empirical investigation does not support this opinion,[31] it is highly probable that there exist only opportunities in this direction rather than actual movements. Nonetheless, production cooperatives such as Cruz Azul, Deeder Cooperative Society, Bhel and Brewery Union revealed a high degree of productivity and efficiency under suitable conditions of participation and self-management which cannot be attributed solely to the technical factors. However, from the analysis of other enterprises in the sample, one cannot conclude that this impact is always present.

Employment Policy in Selected Participatory and Self-Managed Firms

This chapter will deal primarily with the employment policy of these enterprises, and with the public question of the responsiveness of self-managed and participatory enterprises' to market changes in employment. However, it is necessary to take into account that the sample contains a highly heterogeneous structure of enterprises and it is necessary to group them into public enterprises, production cooperatives and Yugoslav-type of enterprises. Essential differences in the employment policy can be identified between these groups of enterprises . It is therefore wise to summarize employment characteristics according to the defined classification of enterprises.

The first characteristic of public enterprises in the sample is the employment of a large number of workers. BHEL, for example, employs 69,800 workers, COMIBOL 27,711 workers, and Sri Lanka Port Authority 21,648 workers. High employment figures can be attributed to technological factors of production or to economies of scale. In this context, two additional factors of over-employment in public enterprises should be mentioned: a tendency for market concentration and thus collection of economic rents; and, soft financing for the majority of public enterprises which link employment policy to a relative availability of cheap financial resources. Not surprisingly it is mentioned that employment is not strictly an economic variable. These enterprises believe that their most important function is to employ workers even in the case of decreased productivity.[32]

These enterprises therefore do not lay off workers in times of crisis. Furthermore, they respond differently than do capitalistic firms in such crisis periods. In Malta Drydocks, due to a long period of difficulties in the shipbuilding industry they introduced various precautions: they decreased the overtime work, they did not lay off workers and did not reduce their basic wages; they did not hire new workers; and, they decreased the number of employees by natural causes such as retirement and free decisions to leave the enterprise. In Sri Lanka Port Authority, when and certain jobs were no longer needed due to improved technology, they reacted similarly.

On the basis of the sample of enterprises one can conclude that public enterprises had a relatively stable level employment in the last decade.[33] With this in mind, some important characteristics of the structure of employed workers can be identified. Due to internal education and training of workers, the qualification structure of workers was highly improved in some enterprises. At the same time, the growth of administrative personnel was evident in almost all enterprises. This may be the result of either technological changes, or, more likely, the result of the growing bureaucratization of management. In COMIBOL for example, the number of workers increased by 8.4%, while the number of administrative workers increased by 17.9% between 1977 to 1984.[34] Job security is the most important task of public enterprises, although it limits their flexibility to manage according to market conditions. Those who advance the most in these enterprises are the groups of workers who are involved in bureaucratic and administrative management.

The production cooperatives which are represented in the sample of enterprises also follow the theoretical predictions of employment policy. They usually do not lay off their members, even during considerable delays in the product sales. The number of employees is adjusted by employing non-members of the cooperative or by varying the number of working hours of the members. Like public enterprises, the production cooperatives reduce workers wages during a crisis,[35] but not under the guaranteed minimum, and they decrease employment in the natural way, such as through retirement and free decisions of workers to leave the enterprise. However, one must bear in mind that the majority of cooperativews were established in order to retain employment and/or preserve land through workers' take-overs.[36] As job security is one of the most important values, members of production cooperatives oppose the firing of members.[37] Job security is also the reason why the possibility of employment of non-members is a very important factor in the efficiency of production cooperatives. Given the economic circumstances, the production cooperatives are flexible in adjusting employment and production through the employment of workers on a contract basis. Furthermore, production cooperatives develop the basis for further recruitment of members. They allow for the employment of workers with special education and qualification when the existing workers are not appropriately qualified. Employment of non-members is a wide spread strategy among production cooperatives in the sample of enterprises. For example, in Cruz Azul 885 members and 511 nonmembers were employed by the end of 1983. A similar strategy was employed in Coope-Silencio and the Deeder Cooperative Society.

The aforementioned production cooperatives have different ways of accepting new members. The Deeder Cooperative Society has the most liberal way of accepting new members: anyone can become a member of the cooperative, regardless of age, sex or religion. Even children are able to become members. Production cooperatives therefore include almost all family members in a village and cover a wide range of activities. A very interesting case of this type is the production cooperative Coope-Silencio. In 1975, the majority of members agreed to employ new members, provided the economic circumstances were favorable. In 1980, only 67% of members were still in favor of employing new members, while 20% of members do not favor new employment, and 13% thought that new employment was unacceptable. This group feared that the new members would only expropriate the benefits earned in the past. In reality the number of members has not increased since 1974, while the number of non-members has. In 1983, the most skilled workers who established the cooperative decided to leave and start private businesses. Each year Cruz Azul the most prospective workers are selected among the candidates for membership.[38] However, they follow the formal rules of: searching among non-members if members within the cooperative do not possess the necessary education and skills;[39] treating education and training of members as an investment and not as a cost; promotion inside the enterprise to serious selection and competition among members. Cruz Azul had the most rational approach to selection of new members among the production cooperatives. However, in Cruz Azul the employment policy also had some defect. Until 1981, the members of this production cooperative did not employ technical personnel because they feared their superiority. When they recognized that this discrimination essentially slowed down their development, they decided to abolish it. From that time on, education became an important goal in this production cooperative and Cruz Azul began to encourage it in various forms.

The employment characteristics of the Yugoslav self-managed enterprises are clearly visible in the Brewery Union case study. The results of the study indicate that the typical Yugoslav enterprise faces various influences on its employment policy: influences from self-management per se; influences which are the consequences of institutional differences in Yugoslavia; influence which are the result of the environment in which self-management operates especially the differences which exist between the regions with a surplus of labor and those with a shortage of labor; and, specific characteristics of individual enterprises' employment. Data collected from this study shows that the number of employees did not vary within a short time period. When they hired new workers they followed the principle of net income maximization for each worker. The data also indicates that the employees' personal income was highest during periods when there was a smaller increase in the number of new employees or when the total number of workers decreased. Workers in the enterprise were reluctant to employ new workers because of the eventual difficulties in firing them. The elasticity of demand of employment was therefore small.

However, employment of new workers in Yugoslav enterprises is a policy which is included in the planning system of the society.[40] This results in a higher employment rate in Yugoslav enterprises than that in enterprises which have total autonomy in employment policy. Due to overemployment, existing enterprises frequently apply monopolistic or oligopolistic pressure to ensure more favorable business conditions, and especially to obtain "cheap" financial sources. Econometric research shows, however, that employment in Yugoslav enterprises lies somewhere in the range between employment typical in a self-managed enterprise and employment of a capitalist enterprise.[41] It also shows that the driving force behind new employment is investment, which, together with technological progress increase the growth of labor productivity of existing workers. Income per worker is also growing as the rate of underpriced financial sources for investments increase.

Yugoslav enterprises do not fire workers. Except in case of serious discipline problems Yugoslav workers rarely lose their jobs. In the case of market expansion, enterprises decide between hiring temporary workers, such as seasonal workers, or increasing working hours. In case of decreasing demand, workers collectively decrease working hours by taking collective holidays, and decrease employment by taking their retirement or by voluntarily leaving the enterprise. In general, however, fluctuation of workers is not an important category and is usually attributed to workers who are retiring. Fluctuation of workers is higher in more developed regions than in less developed regions due to greater employment possibilities.

What can be concluded on the basis of this overview of employment policy in participatory and self-management production units from the sample of enterprises? The joint conclusion is that public enterprises, production cooperatives and Yugoslav self-managed enterprises are considerably inelastic in adjusting employment to changes in market parameters. This includes the employment of new temporary workers or the increase in number of working hours when the market changes require increased production, as well as the possibility for the reduction of employment when they prefer to reduce working hours of all employees and to promote natural leaves rather than laying off workers. None of the introduced groups of enterprises shown above fire workers during short-run disturbances in the market because employment security is one of the most important values of employed workers. Is this the major problem in achieving the efficiency of participatory and self-managed production units? The guarantee of job security, which is commonly connected to "soft budget constraint" in the acquisition of capital as well as to financial nondiscipline and monopolistic and oligopolistic market structure, leads to major breakdowns in the economy and to losses in the gross national product due to allocation and production inefficiency. If an enterprise works under a "hard budget constraint,"[42] rigidity in employment does not have such a negative effect. If the security of employment raises labor productivity the workers attachment to an enterprise contributes to higher efficiency.

Internal Rewards of Workers in the Selected Participatory and Self-Managed Enterprises

Theoretical literature developed three hypotheses about the basic differences between a capitalist and participatory or self-managed enterprise regarding workers' rewards: participatory or self-managed enterprises develop a wider distribution scheme than a capitalist enterprise; the differences in incomes and internal distribution are smaller in participatory and self-managed enterprises than in capitalist ones; and, because of the lack of a labor market, differences between personal income of workers in different enterprises might be larger in self-managed enterprises than those in capitalist firms. The rest of the chapter will include discussions concerning these hypotheses based on research findings.

Schemes of Internal Distribution of Income in the Examined Enterprises. The participatory and self-managed production units which represent the sample of enterprises developed the distribution schemes which not only includes direct payment of workers for their work, in the form of personal incomes. It also consists of various compensations, subsidies and various forms of collective consumption which are given to the workers in the form of different expenses for collective consumption for the improvement of their welfare. Table 4.7 shows the various systems of subsidies and

TABLE 4.7
AN OVERVIEW OF THE SCHEMES OF FRINGE AND WELFARE BENEFITS IN THE ENTERPRISES

ENTERPRISE	BONUSES AND ALLOWANCES	WELFARE BENEFITS AND INCOME IN KIND
COMIBOL	no data	1. Four staple products: sugar, rice, meat and bread available at 1956 prices
BHOPAL UNIT (HEIL)	Cost of living allowance due to inflation house rent allowance: 15% of basic wage city compensatory allowance night-shift allowance transport allowance	1. Education allowance for children 2. Housing for 75% of the total work force with rent 10% of the basic wage/salary 3. Health: 1 clinic with 350 beds, 8 dispensaries, free medical treatment 4. Education: in-plant training, Nindi teaching scheme, adult education for workers 5. Education for children: 5 primary — middle — 2 higher-secondary schools 6. Recreation and welfare: 3 welfare centers, land and religious facilities, sports, cultural activities 7. Bus facilities 8. Aid to families of deceased employees; employee counseling and rehabilitation 9. Assistance to cooperative societies

(continues)

Table 4.7 continued

ENTERPRISE	BONUSES AND ALLOWANCES	WELFARE BENEFITS AND INCOME IN KIND
HARDWARE DIVISION (HEEP)	no data (similar to HEIL)	1. 5394 houses for 50% of workers, new plans: own housing scheme, cooperative housing scheme land, and loans 2. Health: 1 clinic with 170 beds, 8 dispensaries, mobile medicare unit, medical check-up for school children 3. Recreation: parks, playgrounds 4. Transport action subsidies 5. Canteen 6. Social and cultural activities 7. Cooperative society, fair price shops
SONACOB	allowances for: special posts, hard and harmful work, permanent services, tedious work	no data
SRI LANKA PORTS AUTHORITY	work incentives payments, overtime	no data
MALTA DRYDOCKS	no data	no data
NATIONAL BANK OF COMMERCE	housing allowance, sickness allowance, overtime payments	1. Meal coupons, uniforms 2. Remittance funds 3. Transportation 4. Loans to staff 5. Education

Table 4.7 continued

ENTERPRISE	BONUSES AND ALLOWANCES	WELFARE BENEFITS AND INCOME IN KIND
URAFIKI TEXTILE MILL	Incentives, overtime payments	1. Canteen 2. Housing 3.Education: in-plant high school, technical training school 4. Health (clinics, visiting doctors) 5. Sport
CRUZ AZUL	half-month's pay, savings and capital accounts for members paid vacation saving fund, loans, social security payments, retirement payment, retirement fund for non-members, bonus for non-members	1. Housing: housing fund to provide low-cost loans. common model-home, housing cooperative 2. Health: medical services 3. Education: members and children 4. Food: voucher for consumer sector, credit facilities, food-aid for personnel living in Mexico City 5. Life insurance 6. Sporting grounds 7. Cultural services
DEEDER COOPERATIVE SOCIETY	no data	1. Loans to cooperative members 2. Insurance schemes: livestock insurance, group insurance, loss compensatory insurance 3. Health and nutrition: training for health workers, prevention and medical treatment, vaccination, nutritious food

(continues)

Table 4.7 continued

ENTERPRISE	BONUSES AND ALLOWANCES	WELFARE BENFITS AND INCOME IN KIND
ALUMINA	no data	1. Housing: apartments, loans which were far below the needs of workers 2. Vacation houses for workers 3. Education: training of workers, scholarships 4. Rising outlays for common consumption
BREWERY UNION	overtime & night shift payments, individual & collective performance bonuses (incentives), rewards for work anniversaries and a retirement reward	1. Canteen (almost free) 2. Leave reimbursement, holiday facilities at subsidized prices 3. Kindergarten 4. Transport reimbursement 5. Workers' education 6. One monthly case of beer at lower prices. 7. Housing: large number of individual apartments, present-day housing loans at very low interest rate
INDUSTRY OF MOTORS RAKOVICA	no data	1. Workers' canteen

compensations for work done and expenses for collective consumption which were developed in the enterprises under study. Once again, the methodology of separating the enterprises into public enterprises, production cooperatives and Yugoslav enterprises will be used . In addition the characteristics of the distribution schemes will be analyzed according to each group of enterprise.

The distribution schemes which include the system of personal income, different compensations and various forms of collective consumption are presents in public enterprises which belong to this sample of enterprises, especially in countries with some form of industrial tradition. For example in India the data from the study of BHEL shows that workers in this enterprise received bonuses which were not related to payment from their personal income.[43] It is important to distinguish between the standard program of collective consumption, such as health and education, from other expenses for collective consumption which are given to workers. In COMIBOL, for example, the four staple products: sugar, rice, meat and bread were available to workers in 1956 prices. In this way, workers real wages did not diminish in the period of crisis although real money wages fell.[44] Similar distribution were also developed in other public enterprises, as in the National Bank of Commerce, in Urafiki Textile Mill[45] and ROP Limited.[46]

Production cooperatives such as Cruz Azul, Deeder Cooperative Society and Coope Silencio formed a similar system of distribution. Cruz Azul is a special case. Not only is it a concrete industry, but it has developed various other activities as well, such as construction, a housing cooperative, transportation, exploration of raw materials, two agriculture cooperatives, a sports club, a shopping center, a medical center and other services for the community where the factory is located. Some cooperatives were established for the regulation of employment and economic activity such as exploration of raw materials, transport cooperative, agriculture units, and services. Meanwhile others were established for activities such as medical services, schools, recreational and cultural services to provide for the well being of cooperative members and to give stimulus to the whole cooperative movement. In effect, Cruz Azul is a country within a country, which on the social basis, succeeded in integrations an important segment of people into an efficient socio-economic entity.

Yugoslav enterprises have a system of benefits and allowances for the collective consumption of their workers which was developed in great detail and regulated by law. It is important to note that the system has been evolving throughout the post-war period with a constant tendency to evaluate both the collective as well as the individual contribution of each member. Therefore, in time the share of basic personal income decreased while the importance of individual contribution increased. Contributions differed among various groups of workers. Numerous allowances for working conditions such as night work, shift work, length of service in one enterprise and stimulation for business success have gained importance. In 1982 for example, the structure of average personal incomes in the Brewery Union was as follows: 66.3% was the normative personal income for actual effective work;[47] 2.2% was the allowance for night and shift work; 6.1% was the reward for effective management of past labor and length of service in the Brewery Union; 5.7% was rewarded for business success which greatly varied during the year; 11% were subsidies for annual leave, holidays and other allowed absences from work; 4.7% were sick leave payments borne by the Brewery Union such as a maximum of one-month sick leave and a portion of maternity leave payments; 2.7% were children allowances and transportation subsidies; 1.3% was overtime payment.

Aside from bonuses and allowances contained in their personal incomes, the Yugoslav workers enjoy a relatively high degree of collective consumption financed, by their incomes.[48] Part of the incomes is paid by enterprises into the collective consumption fund which is intended for direct consumption by workers in the enterprises. Since the distribution of income among personal incomes of members of the enterprise is often restricted by various formal and informal contracts and agreements regarding the distribution of income and personal incomes, workers of an enterprise, especially in the more successful enterprises, prefer to replace their right of income distribution with their right of collective consumption.[49] For example, Brewery Union has four vacation homes, a building for kindergarten, and a kitchen where workers are given warm meals. It organizes various education courses for its workers and 48.2% of workers live in apartments owned by the Brewery. In one form or another, the Brewery has helped solve the housing problem of 3/5 of its workers.

Internal Distribution of Income and Its Inequalities. Vanek (1970) leaves it to the workers of individual enterprises to find the right formula for the fairest distribution of the personal income fund among workers. However, Williamson (1980) disagrees with him. He believes that self-managed and participatory enterprises, using the system where the level of personal incomes is based on realized income, lack the criteria for internal distribution of income since there is no labor market. Sertel (1984) has developed a model related to this in which the criteria for formulation of payment for one unit of individual work effort is determined. Payment in this model is based on work done. If the collective consumption of workers based on the distribution by need is inserted into this model, the system approaches the Yugoslav system of enterprises.[50] The question about incentive of workers arises.[51] However, before attempting to answer this, one should look at how the problem of internal distribution of income was solved in the public enterprises and production cooperatives which form our sample of enterprises.

Some public enterprises have devoted considerable time to the problem of internal distribution. The management structure of BHEL totally re-evaluated the criteria for rewarding workers while inviting various workers' bodies to participate in this re-evaluation. They developed a system while incorporate various subsidies and compensations, such as the bonus system.[52] SONACOB has evolved a profit-sharing system which determines the incomes of workers according to their results in production. Personal incomes of workers consist of basic wages, additional payment for individual physical productivity (0 - 10% of basic wage) and additional payment for collective productivity (0 - 30% of basic wage).

A special distribution scheme has also been evolved in some production cooperatives in which capital accounts are introduced in addition to wages for work done. Cruz Azul has the most elaborate system which is very similar to the system of income distribution in the known case of the Mondragon production cooperatives. Based on the starting share of a member of the production cooperative, a capital account is opened for each member at a 6% annual rate of interest. From time to time the account is revalued because of inflation and increased annually by allocating a portion of the income of the cooperative into the Members' accounts.[53] The members who leave the cooperative have the right to withdraw their savings from the capital account. The workers in Cruz Azul therefore receive three kinds of current income: basic wage; interest on individual capital accounts; bonuses, and, allowances and funds for collective consumption. The system of determining basic wages is fairly complicated and is being reformulated. The ratio between the lowest and the highest basic wages of workers is 1 : 24 which is very high for production cooperatives. Nevertheless, it is considerably less than in other Mexican enterprises.

Coope-Silencio does not have a system of capital accounts for its members, however, the profit is distributed among the workers at the end of the year in accordance with the amount of labor. In Deeder Cooperative only a minor share of profit is given to shareholders as dividends, the majority is re-invested or put into various funds of collective consumption and used by all workers. Because the workers joined the cooperative at different times, their shares vary as well. For example 6% of the richest members of the cooperative receive more than 20% of all dividends. This is not looked upon unfavorably by other members since the richest (and the oldest) members significantly contribute to funding of common consumption funds.

Yugoslav enterprises have developed different profit-sharing formulas. As was seen in the case of Brewery Union, in 1982 about 5.7% of the average personal income of the worker was calculated on the basis of business result. Meanwhile, the share of individual contribution was calculated on the basis of physical productivity which can be measured for groups of workers or even individuals, and which forms part of his basic personal income. In this distribution, there is a special category of past labor which can be described as the basis for capital accounts in Cruz Azul. Although the idea of past labor was primarily intended to increase the interest of the worker to manage social capital, its implementation did not produce the anticipated results. It was intended to to be an improvement in three regards: as a measure for distribution of the total revenue in the case of applied principle of joint revenue; as a substitute for joint resources in case of applied principle of joint income;[54] and, as an element of internal distribution of income among members of the enterprise. Its application in the Yugoslav practice did not significantly influence self-financing of investments or increase effectiveness of investments. It influenced the formulation of personal incomes of workers only when the principle of seniority was applied.

As the inequality in distribution among workers of one enterprise is analyzed ,it should be stressed that it was impossible to make a comparative analysis in the sample enterprises because of the scarcity of data for the majority of the enterprises. However, there is certain qualitative data on inequality, e.g., in Coope-Silencio the management board members receive no additional pay for performing that function. The pay for regular and overtime work is the same. In Cruz Azul, there is no difference between both factories in salaries for equal work. There are also few differences in the payment for equal work between members and non-members of the cooperative. BHEL has a unified structure for the entire corporation. In Malta Drydocks, differences in personal incomes of the workers are relatively small and workers consider them just.

An exact analysis of inequalities in income distribution was made in the Brewery Union where different criteria for inequality reveal that there was relative egalitarian distribution during the whole period (the ratio between the highest and the lowest personal incomes of the workers was the largest in 1961 = 2.96, and the smallest in 1965 = 1.91). In 1982 the value of Gini's inequality index was 0.165. The comparison with the rest of the food industry, where the value of Gini's inequality index was 0.168, shows that there was relatively even distribution in the Yugoslav economy as a whole. A comparison with Western European firms, however, shows that in Yugoslav enterprises skilled workers and managers earn less than their colleagues in capitalist enterprises. The existing institutional setting thus represents a dilemma for public policy. It is frequently argued that the dispersion of personal incomes, especially across skill groups, is too small to provide satisfactory incentives for optimal effort and quantity of work by workers. Yet, the opinions of the majority of workers and the established system of decision making have a strong tendency to favor a more narrow range in the distribution of personal incomes.

Differences in Personal Incomes for Equal Work Among Workers in Different Work Organizations. Ward (1958) and Meade (1972) point to significant differences which may emerge in payments for equal work among individual work organizations since a self-managing economy has no labor market which would equate the payment of a worker with the value of his marginal product. Because of this, enterprises will not employ new workers beyond the point at which the income per worker would become equal to the value of his marginal product. Thus, the economy would not reach Pareto's optimum.[55]

On the basis of the analysis of the data, it is impossible to assess the 'deficiency' of a self-managed economy. Data shows that the analyzed enterprises have higher personal incomes than do the national economies as a whole.[56] It was however impossible to make comparative studies of personal incomes of workers employed in self-managing enterprises with those employed in individual countries.

The only example in this area, albeit incomplete, is given by data on inter-enterprise differences in personal incomes for equal work in Yugoslavia. But there are a number of studies which explain that there are a number of institutional peculiarities and administrative limitations in Yugoslavia which enable the enterprises to take advantage of economic and monopolistic situations. Thus, the difference in incomes for equal work among different enterprises can hardly be attributed solely to imperfections arising out of the non-existence of a labor market. Some signs also point out that the introducing of institutional opportunities for the implementation of income per worker as the basic economic goal would lead to the problems described earlier.[57] It is likely that the total liberation of the distribution of income in enterprises, even when taking into account the so-called equal conditions, would lead to greater differences in pay for equal work in individual enterprises. This is due to the differences that would certainly arise from the deficiencies due to the non-existence of a labor market in the real Yugoslav economy.

Financing of Enterprises Under Review

Economic literature focuses primarily on two problems related to the financing of self-managed enterprises and their financial decisions. What will be the financial investments of a self-managed enterprise in comparison to a capitalist (neoclassical) enterprise (compared to capitalist enterprise, how will the self-managed enterprise grow). And, how will the self-managed enterprise finance its investments. With regard to the first problem, the theory explains that the self-managed enterprise will grow more slowly than the capitalist one. With regard to the second problem, it expresses several doubts about the possibilities of efficient financing of investments in a self-managed enterprise, especially when taking into account the problem of risk-taking. As mentioned above, the characteristics of the Yugoslav concept of social property represent a special problem in the financing of Yugoslav self-managed enterprises.

The question is raised about the importance of the above conclusions in the case of public enterprises, production cooperatives and Yugoslav enterprises represented in the sample. The sample of these enterprises is very heterogeneous while the case study methodology used was not adequate to test these and similar assumptions; it is therefore impossible to reach any firm conclusions which would confirm or reject the results of the model. However, on the basis of data collected it is nevertheless possible to arrive at some facts which could be used as practical information in conceptualizing further theoretical and empirical work.

As far as the optimal size of a self-managed enterprise is concerned, the data shows in general that public enterprises in the sample are not problematic from the lack of size, but from excessive size, both of employees and of the capital they are managing. The questions of how much they exceed optimal size, why they are exceed it and how this arises, are much more important in this regard.[58] The same questions can also be posed when considering production cooperatives in the sample. For example, Cruz Azul is larger than the average Mexican concrete factory, and is a specimen of stable growth over a longer period.[59] Similar conclusions are also valid for Coope-Silencio and Deeder Cooperative Society but not for the Contex production cooperative. Finally, the same is true for Yugoslav enterprises as well. For example, the study of the Brewery Union shows that it is near in size to larger breweries in Western Europe but that it does not operate above their average costs. The study also shows a normal and stable growth of the enterprise over a longer period of time which is, in the authors' opinion, largely related to some kind of agreement between the enterprise and the representatives of local authorities with regard to a tax on the product which enabled a normal expansion of production in the brewery.

As a rule, the larger than optimal size of the enterprise is related to the manner of financing of public enterprises. Data on the amount of subsidies received by the enterprises through direct subsidies, loans with lower interest rates, tax reductions or pricing policy is not available. However, a detailed analysis would certainly reveal this. Thus this study cannot show systematic characteristics of financing of public enterprises which would help the analysis.

A more precise picture is given by the data on financing of production cooperatives which is included in the sample. It should first be noted that the financial analysis of Cruz Azul does not confirm to the general consensus that workers would prefer to invest their savings in a broad portfolio of shares, and thus lessen the risk of their investment[60] than to invest in the production cooperative. The same financial analysis also negates the existence of the well-known Furobotn-Pejovich effect according to which workers will prefer to open their own personal savings accounts rather than invest in their enterprise. And finally, Cruz Azul offers no support to the thesis that, with the growth of a self-managed enterprise, old workers would forfeit their privileged position in the enterprise and thus refuse to employ new workers. On the whole, Cruz Azul is an example of a successful production cooperative for which no argument usually tendered by the critics of participatory and self-managed production forms is valid. The system of capital accounts described in the previous chapter ensures the distribution of risk among the members of the cooperative on the basis of their private ownership of part of the means of production. Since it operates in accordance with the Mexican law on production cooperatives, it must distribute 7% of total income into the so-called social fund[61] which also represents the cooperative's own resources or equity, thus giving the opportunity to counterbalance business risk. Aside from this, the members also contribute other additional resources necessary for financing the growth of the cooperative and for satisfying the various needs of the broader community. The following are the reasons for doing so, according to the study:

1. By not investing they would lose market share, production capacity would not be fully utilized and the quality of cement would be lower than that of their competitors;
2. By not investing there would be no employment of new workers and the general well-being of the commune's members would be lower;
3. The benefits from investing into production capacity, such as employment for family members, better social services, establishment of capital accounts for future needs, and better regional prosperity in an economic, social and cultural sense, are far greater than returns from alternative investments.

Since Cruz Azul operates within normal market conditions, the collective savings are the result of a survival instinct of its workers.[62] It is important to warn that in the isolated cooperative movement such as in the Mondragon system the members of the cooperative value the stability of employment highly and view the preservation of current market conditions as necessary factors for the preservation of the movement. It would thus be incorrect to generalize the success of all production cooperatives and self-managed enterprises based on example.[63] Savings of members in Coope Silencio, for example, is defined by legal procedures for the division of net income.[64] Overwhelming savings of workers in Deeder Cooperative Society are based on their huge sacrifice of current consumption. These two examples are isolated cases as well, which do not entirely reflect[65] all the examples in the world, especially not the characteristics of wider self-managed movement.[66]

In this regard, the Yugoslav economy is the best case for testing the models' conclusions. To some extent, one would agree with Horvat[67] that the events in the Yugoslav economy during the last ten years are beyond any normal economic reasoning and thus, one would be unable to draw a conclusion about the power of any model of a self-managed economy. However, it is also true that although empirical investigations for the period before the 70s show a reasonable rate of savings of Yugoslav self-managed enterprises,[68] the results cannot avoid the fact that the marginal propensity to save of Yugoslav enterprises is very low.[69] Underdeveloped financial markets and the reasons mentioned above force the banking system to "produce" enough loans to cover the financing of selected investment priorities. The soft budget constraint is therefore the result of an incomplete system of financing investments in the Yugoslav context [70] and to some degree, reflects the problems mentioned at the beginning of the chapter. The low marginal propensity to save of enterprises,[71] however, requires the interference of state and para-statal institutions in decision-making in enterprises. On the other hand, the financial system operates in a manner that penalizes the decisions that were approved without demonstrating their economic effects. Some enterprises borrow money which is not repaid in real value due to an inappropriate accounting system. Others do not repay its nominal value due to a failure in paying back loans and interests, to the conversion of short-term emission loans into long-term loans, or to the formation of the institution of so-called exchange rate differences. Commercial enterprises' losses are taken over by banks and the National Bank of Yugoslavia covers their losses.

At this moment, one of the key requirements of the reform of the Yugoslav economy is the establishment of necessary conditions for the normal operation of its financial system. A capital account of workers is the solution for the Mondragon cooperative system and for Cruz Azul in Mexico, representing one of the options in this system. On the basis of workers' personal property rights on capital accounts, it also guarantees the distribution of risk between members of an enterprise. However, in this regard, Gui (1985) accurately reasons that the capability of financing their activity on the basis of the individual capital accounts is limited. It is therefore necessary that enterprises appear on the capital market as demanders for additional short-term or long-term financial sources. The share of individual workers' property is an indicator to external financial institutions, or banks, of workers' losses if an enterprise goes bankrupt. On the basis of this indicator which shows the financial power of an enterprise, financial institutions are willing to participate in financing the activity. Private information becomes public and external financial institutions such as banks become involved in decision-making in an enterprise. In this case the model of self-managed decision-making is essentially transformed into the model of co-determination.

If one relates these thoughts to the discussion of the nature of decision-making processes and of distribution processes in the enterprises interviewed, one questions the extent to which the nature of decision-making processes is changed if instruments which enterprises use in developed market economies to form equity are introduced. In this regard, Meade's model of worker-capital discriminatory partnership (1972) removes various gaps, found in the Ward-Vanek self-managed economy.[72] However,[73] Meade's model refers back to the labor market. Nuti (1988) partially corrects this model with the introduction of a requirement that shares from the retained earnings are equally owned solely by members of the enterprise (workers' partnership.) They can be cashed at any time; new workers purchase them from old workers. Members of an enterprise and hired workers should generally have an equal vote in decision-making. Only members of an enterprise will make decisions about the reinvestment of income. If one allows the formation of capital shares owned by members of an enterprise and if these shares are issued without limitations for each member, one can evaluate an enterprise without the establishment of a highly developed capital market. Shares will become a subject of sale between members of an enterprise. If somebody wants to sell his shares at given prices and other members are not willing to buy them, then he will have the right to purchase shares from members at given price.

Nuti still preserves the role of self-managed decision-making but he introduces new characteristics into the field of workers' saving in enterprises. Although his model is applied to the present situation in the Yugoslav economy, it is questionable if the suggested changes serve the fulfillment of higher allocative and productive efficiency of the Yugoslav economy. Financing to stimulate the productive savings of individuals and enterprises, as well as the rational investment of savings are needed. From the standpoint of the national economy, it must not only include workers' savings and productive investments or workers' shares within an enterprise, but also the flow of savings from cells with excessive funds to deficit cells, taking into account their opposite interests, such as capital shares. Nuti's model therefore considers the mechanical composition of members' interests in an enterprise and does not consider the establishment of the entire market adjustment of interests between particular subjects in the entire national economy, such as labor markets and capital market.

Entry of New Enterprises into the Market Structure

In the second chapter, different explanations for the entry of new participatory and self-managed enterprises in the market structure as well as supporting organizations which will stimulate entry of new enterprises were developed. However, this discussion was concerned with the theoretical model of the self-managed economy.

Based on the discussions in this book, it would be pointless to emphasize the importance of the entry of self-managed firms as a condition for macroeconomic stability in the countries studied. No country investigated gives an example of successful implementation of self-management and participation at the macro level. However, there is support for the success of participation and self-management at the micro level. The following questions therefore arise concerning developing and socialist economies: What should the developing countries do with an inefficient public sector which is the result of extensive development in the sixties and seventies? What should be done within the socialist economies which lack small and middle-sized enterprises, and which deal with inefficient, large state- owned enterprises which were stimulated by preceding economic policies? Reconstruction of the inefficient social or public sector with different privatization schemes and the stimulation of new entry seem to be proper answer to these questions.[74] Moreover, it can be argued that with a suitable combination of the aforementioned ways of management of the economy, which will also include some form of workers' participation, better economic and social effects will be achieved.

Notes

1. See Pryor (1983)
2. Such examples of public firms are: COMIBOL, Bolivia; BHEL, India; Bhopal Unit, India; Hardwar Division, India; Malta Drydocks, Malta; Sri Lanka Ports Authority Sri Lanka; National Bank of Commerce, Tanzania; Urafaki Textile Mill Ltd., Tanzania; and, SONACOB, Algeria.
3. CONTEX was built as a private firm in 1947. As a result of the General Law of Industry in 1974, the owners wanted to move the enterprise to another location. Strongly opposing this, workers borrowed money and took over the private firm. In 1980 workers changed the firm into a productive cooperative.
4. In 1978, minerals represented 71% of the export, in 1984 only 45.5. Since production continued to decrease, exports fell again in 1986.
5. BHEL is among the ten biggest producers of electrical equipment in the world.
6. A typical example in this direction is Deeder Cooperative Society in Bangladesh. It developed banking (collecting and investing free financial resources), production (production programs were changed several times), insurance and enormous social programs for the development of the commune.
7. Cruz Azul in Mexico is a good example of this kind of cooperative organization which provides higher employment than the basic production unit does. A similar idea was also developed in BHEL, which: a) helps cooperatives to fulfill some needs of their workers such as housing, food, trade; and, b) helps to bring to life the inefficient public enterprises from Karnataka.
8. A typical example in this direction is SONACOB. It is less important for ROP Limited (Zambia) which is supervised by the Industrial Development Cooperation (INDECO).

9. I.e., either the direct decisions of workers or the decisions through their delegates.
10. However, the empirical studies of Yugoslav firms show that this goal is one of the most important ones in the structure of goals of Yugoslav workers. See Prasnikar (1983) and Prasnikar and Svejnar (1988).
11. The discussion is presented in Vahcic (1982)
12. See Horvat (1982), Pucko (1986) for a more detailed discussion.
13. Various opinions on ways to provide this distribution exist. Adisez (1969) defined self-management as the strategic decision-making process, and leadership as the administrative, executive and tactical decision-making process. Zupanov (1969) discussed professionalization of the managerial activity which interferes with management. Firstly, it interferes with the establishments of concrete relations with external units as well as with the leadership of the enterprise. Secondly, it interferes with the regulation of relations within and among units. Self-management interferes partially with the acceptance of strategic decisions and with workers' decision-making in working groups. This decision-making involves personal incomes working conditions, hiring and firing of workers, and the balance of interests between institutionalized units and interest groups. In this way, the oligarchic distribution of power in decision-making is formed and workers must be organized into unions to try to provide the fulfillment of their requirements through strikes. However, in this way it is possible to establish economic efficiency and democratic influence of workers in decision-making. Horvat (1982) discusses strategic decisions which are accepted by the workers' assembly, tactical decisions which are accepted by the managerial board, professional decisions made by experts and, finally the routine decisions which are fulfilled by the administration. Goldstein (1985) proclaims workers' assembly as the basic power. The manager is responsible for the fulfillment of the collective business function and who executes the strategic decisions of the workers' assembly. The workers' council is the executive body of the workers' assembly, which makes the necessary decisions for the manager to execute the business function.
14. In a typical public enterprise such as Comibol, BHEL, Malta Drydocks, Sri Lanka Port Authority, National Bank of Commerce, Urafiki Textile Mills Ltd., ROP Limited and Sonacob this relation exists in the managerial context. The managerial workers are usually government staff. Otherwise, they are promoted by the government or execute government orders. The government directs the enterprise through various measures of pricing, investment, financial, union, personal and foreign trade policy, as can be seen in Sonacob, Malta Drydocks and Sri Lanka Port Authority. It also happens that the enterprises execute special tasks which are designated by the government as in the National Bank of Commerce. Also some of the cooperative enterprises are tied to the government and to the fulfillment of their goals as in Coope Silencio, Contex, Deeder Cooperative Society and Grameen Bank. The relation between the Yugoslav enterprises and the state and parastatal institutions was not revealed in the direct paternalistic role of the government, rather in unstable economic conditions which were linked to the fulfillment of political and social goals. Although this relation changed over time, the framework of these restrictions made the Yugoslav enterprises somehow more independent than typical public enterprises.

15. For example the Brewery Union had economic units which were introduced at the end of fifties and which were later abolished due to overwhelming freedom. In 1963, they were replaced by working units. The working units were broader than the economic units and with all the self-management functions, preserved the business unity of the enterprises. BOALs, which were introduced in the seventies, reflect the anticipation of the previous period. However, the BOALs were given the status of a legal subject and this had the possibility to lead business policy which was not necessarily adjusted to the policy of the entire enterprise.
16. This considers neither the pressure of unsuitable economic conditions (connected to the unsuitable construction of the economic system and to unbalanced measures of economic policy) on the decisions of the Yugoslav enterprises, nor the continuous normative changes of the organization structure of the enterprise and decision-making procedures.
17. The same finding is valid for the Mondragon cooperative movement.
18. It must be noted that new legislation substantially changed these relations.
19. See Zupanov (1969), Obradovic (1974), Arzensek (1974).
20. If we divide the process of decision-making in terms of: initialization of decisions; determination of decision goals; professional preparation of decisions; decision-making; and, execution of decisions. The importance of managerial workers is very high in all but in the fourth phase.
21. The opinion of the national unions on cooperatives is very important. In Mexico for example, the unions oppose the introduction of cooperatives. They believe that it is a revisionist concept which will eventually decrease their own bargaining power.
22. On the involvement of union organizations in the management of the Yugoslav enterprises, see Prasnikar, Svejnar (1988).
23. Zupanov (1969) therefore discusses the professionalization of management.
24. Only a case study of the Brewery Union followed entirely the methodological framework as prepared by Vahcic (1982) and Kavcic (1983).
25. See for example the reports about the operation of Sri Lanka Ports Authority and about the working of Brewery Union.
26. The study mentioned that the decrease of the production in COMIBOL could not be attributed entirely to the introduction of self-management, rather to the decrease in the price of minerals and to general political and economic crisis in Bolivia.
27. Prasnikar and Svejnar (1988) discuss the systemic economic and political factors in Yugoslavia. The two systemic factors result from the operation of labor-managed firm where, income-maximizing workers-members tend to use a higher capital-labor ratio in the presence of rents or extra profits that they appropriate as workers' income; and, operational managers view capital accumulation and firm growth as a means to advance their careers and status. The three policy factors are: the easy access to capital at artificially low cost for many existing firms; an institutional environment that reduces or eliminates the firms ability to lay off or discharge workers; and, the imposition of many enterprise taxes on gross personal incomes or "wages."
28. See Petrin (1981)
29. See Prasnikar, Svejnar (1988) for a more detailed discussion.
30. Typical examples are COMIBOL and Contex.

31. There exist only qualitative signs about the possible correlation. In Heil, a sector of Bhopal, almost all workers and management responded in this direction. In Heep, positive answers were found among workers and management who were members of self-managed bodies; workers-nonmembers also supported this opinion, while only 45% of management-nonmembers support this view. In Malta Drydocks, 69% of workers answered that there exists a positive link between the degree of self-management and higher labor productivity.
32. Since nationalization in 1952, COMIBOL has increased the number of employees from 24,000 to 36,000, although in the meantime, productivity has drastically fallen while the problems of working discipline has increased. In the Malta Drydocks case study, the authors concluded that the shipbuilding factory was in a worse position than the private one, especially since it had to ensure employee job security.
33. The number of employees did not drastically change in the following firms: HEIL, Malta Drydocks, Sri Lanka Ports Authority, Urafiki Textile Mill, ROP Limited. In the case of ROP Limited the state agency (INDECO) required that employees be kept even during a drastic reduction of production. In COMIBOL, they increased the number of employees even though production had fallen.
34. In both units of BHEL, the number of management workers and supervisors increased while the number of unskilled workers decreased. In ROP Limited, newly employed workers in the firm had higher than average education.
35. Estrin (1987) presents three reasons why production cooperatives overcome a crisis more easily than do capitalistic firms: cooperatives can give lower incomes to their members than can capitalistic firms which are bound by union agreements; workers in production cooperatives have developed a higher cooperative spirit; and, production cooperatives are capable of surviving when capitalist firms are not.
36. Cruz Azul, Coope-Silencio and Contex are examples of these types of production cooperatives.
37. The employment of members is, for example, the most important value in Cruz Azul. Here the employment of its members increased independently even at the expense of decreasing productivity. They employed 20% more workers in maintenance and repairs for a limited period only to employ them later for an unlimited period of time so that they could to become members of this production cooperative.
38. Temporarily employed workers who have been offered a particular job were obligated to obtain a permanent contract if they wished to become members of the production cooperatives. Almost 100% of temporary employed workers in Hidalgo and Lagunas wished to become permanent members to ensure their own job security, permanent income and the capitalization of their income.
39. This has proven to be typical way of selecting employees in the successful cooperatives.
40. For more details see Prasnikar and Svejnar (1988)
41. For more details see Prasnikar and Svejnar (1988)
42. This is a specific characteristic of some production cooperatives, such as Cruz Azul, and of various small and medium-sized Yugoslav enterprises such as Brewery Union.

43. In the example HEIL, in the Bhopal Unit free medical care was available to workers and their families, as were five elementary schools, three middle schools, two colleges, three month-long courses for the additional education of workers, evening schools, and housing for 75% of workers.
44. In the period 1980-1984, real money wages fell by 23% while the share of income in kind increased: in 1979 it represented 11% of wages; in 1980, 20%, in 1983, 60%; and, in 1984-1985 over 90%.
45. The following subsidies and compensations exist in the National Bank of Commerce: food stamps, housing, compensations' work uniforms, cost of transportation; and, overtime work. In Urafiki Textile Mill, the distribution scheme includes: meals, housing construction, education; stimulative portion of income, overtime payments; special rewards for the workers who are employed for more than 10 years; and, various loans.
46. In ROP Limited workers paid only 30% of the price in the restaurants; the enterprise had its own transportation; and, 65% of workers lived in apartments owned by the enterprise, and received a housing compensation of 20% of their wage.
47. The number of points in each worker's normative personal income was determined by analytical evaluation of jobs and tasks performed by the worker. This evaluation was done uniformly for the whole brewery while the current value of the points which depend on business results determined the actual amount of money.
48. This is the share of income which workers allocated to special funds in the form of contributions from their wages and personal incomes. These are to ensure the implementation of medical, pension, educational, cultural and other programs.
49. There has been a tendency in Yugoslavia for the distribution of income for collective consumption to be left to individual enterprises. This sometimes resulted in significant differences among individual enterprises and in a renewed tendency to regulate this distribution. It is important to clarify a certain misconception of the term "collective consumption." In Yugoslav enterprises, the distribution of collective consumption consists primarily of allocation to a housing fund, to annual leave and recreation funds, to a subsidy of workers' canteen, and to medical care, among others. The majority of these funds are used to provide housing for workers (the enterprise either buys an apartment or gives loans on acquired terms). Houses and apartments so acquired in this way are then treated as private property and therefore not considered as "collective consumption." Since these resources had been transformed into assets, it would better to define the allocation of housing loans and apartments as income in nature given to workers who live in an apartment bought by enterprise funds or who are given a housing loan with a highly subsidized interest rate. The subsidized use of recreational facilities and homes holiday should be treated similarly. This is also income in kind distributed among workers who use these facilities.
50. It also satisfies the demands put forth by Sen (1966) about the necessity of combining the distribution by labor with the distribution by needs.
51. This question is asked by Jensen, Meckling (1979), Alchian, Demsetz (1972) and Williamson (1980).
52. The system in BHEL consists of: basic wage, compensation for inflation, housing allowance (15% of the basic wage), subsidies for living in town, cleaning of work clothes, transportation, education of children excluded from BHEL's own educational

system, and a system of bonuses which includes rewards for successful individual and business performance.

53. A portion of income is distributed among individual member's accounts according to the following formula: 34% according to the number of working hours, and 66% according to the level of personal incomes of workers.

54. For more about this see in Prasnikar, Svejnar (1988).

55. To solve this problem, Meade proposes the introduction of shares which would differ among members based on the length of their service (workers' shares) and the possibility of issuing capital shares (external shares). The issuing of shares Nuti, (1988) limits this to the members of the organization with the option that members themselves decide whether they will have fixed income, and whether and how much profit they will distribute in the form of shares.

56. Personal incomes of workers in BHEL are the highest in the Indian public sector. The same is true for workers in Malta Drydocks and in Cruz Azul and Coope-Silencio. Personal incomes in Brewery Union are about 20% higher than average personal incomes in the Republic of Slovenia, while workers' incomes in Alumina are higher than average personal incomes of workers in the Republic of Macedonia. The case study of COMIBOL alone states that salaries of miners are lower than the average salaries of workers in other economic branches in Bolivia.

57. The study of the Brewery Union which analyzes this enterprise in detail during the period 1947 to 1982 suggests that the following could happen: (1) in the 60s when the Yugoslav economy was the most market-oriented, the personal incomes of workers in the Brewery Union differed most with the average in the Republic of Slovenia; (2) when economic unities which linked personal incomes to the realized incomes of economic units, were introduced in 1959-1963, a significant fall in employment occurred; (3) data shows that throughout the period, a group of workers with the longest service in the brewery directed the distribution of collective consumption funds, such as housing loans, and construction of week-end houses in their own favor.

58. There is no direct data on this, only indirect information supporting the point of view mentioned above. Employment policy and the highest possible level of employment are clearly one of the most important goals of public enterprises. It is also evident that some public enterprises in the sample have special schemes for raising loans and therefore need not compete for them on the market. They obtain financial resources on the basis of different priority criteria usually are established by government institutions.

59. The Cruz Azul case study shows that it uses very modern technology. Productivity is greater than in the rest of the cement industry and costs per unit are lower. It manages to finance its development with its own financial resources.

60. See Jensen, Meckling (1979), Dreze (1976), Ross (1974).

61. This is more than corporation tax paid by private firms.

62. This argument is also used by Horvat (1986).

63. It must be noted that, in the past, investments in Cruz Azul were also accomplished based on current consumption. New generations of members place higher importance on economic means for stimulating savings also based on functional participation.

64. According to the law, almost 46% of net income must be saved: production investments (15%), obligatory reserves (10%), collective consumption fund (6%), state fund for self-managed cooperatives (5%), financing of unions (5%), fund for education (4%), state cooperative council (1%).
65. The counter example of shipbuilding Malta Drydocks is a typical one related to this. Eighty-three percent of workers interviewed express willingness to increase their effort for reviving the shipbuilding company and pledged not to demand the increase of personal incomes if this were to endanger the development of this enterprise. However, according to the union's tradition of "bargaining," workers rejected the proposal to compensate the enterprise's current losses by a reduction of their wages, even though their wages are among the best in the industry sector of Malta. Similar results are also found in Yugoslavia, where 3000 workers from 147 enterprises were interviewed and more then 50% answered that they were not willing to give up their personal incomes for investments in their enterprises (Prasnikar, 1983).
66. This refers to a self-managed economy which is not an isolated cooperative movement but is included in the entire network of the national economy, or is organized like a national economy as in ths Yugoslavia. In this case, the workers'the time horizon is absolutely shorter and employment in the same enterprise is not their priority because of the employment opportunities which exist in other enterprises.
67. See Horvat (1986).
68. See Miovic (1975) and Tyson (1977).
69. Mitchel (1987) proved that in the existing institutional framework in which Yugoslav enterprises operate, one can identify a suitable degree of savings of enterprises only if reasonable restrictions exist in payment of personal incomes and if a reasonably high demand for the producers' products exist. If the restrictions in distribution of loans exist and if the period of repayment of debt is not the same as the lifetime of capital, the Yugoslav enterprise will invest less than will the capitalist one.
70. See for example Ribnikar (1989), Prasnikar, Svejnar (1988).
71. For more about this, see Prasnikar (1983), Prasnikar, Svejnar (1988).
72. It especially removes the well known Furobotn-Pejovich effect with the opportunity to invest in capital shares in a workers' enterprise and the possibility of co-determination for the owners of capital. See Nuti, (1988).
73. The labor market, is adjusted with important additions such as, employment stability (life-time employment), introduction of seniority rule, introduction of profit-sharing and the role of co-determination.
74. See Prasnikar (1990)

5

Conclusions

1. The growing theoretical and empirical literature on workers' participation and self-management suggest several reasons why participation and self-management in production are conducive to socioeconomic change and economic development in developing countries. These findings can be classified into three groups. First, participation and self-management are considered fundamental to the freedom and fulfillment of humankind. It implies equality in decision-making (concerning production itself and the distribution of surplus), which promotes political freedom, and which emphasizes the individual as an active political being. Second, it has been found that some degree of workers' participation in production is common among firms. This reflects a convergence of different socioeconomic systems and orders in the contemporary world. The third set of findings pertains solely to developing countries after liberation took place in the last few decades. Developing countries are characterized by a traditional hierarchical social structure and an economic system inherited from colonialist rulers. However, participation and self-management can be valuable tools for mobilizing people to bring about social and economic change as well as for stimulating their creative energy.

2. After independence, the majority of developing countries studied in this book implemented workers' participation and self-management as one of their basic development goals. Prior to liberation, there were already some forms of workers' participation in most of these countries. Primarily, there were two early forms: either participation was established in the framework of the Philosophy of Industrial Peace or it was developed in the framework of producer cooperative movements. In the first case, the data shows that the legalization of participation and self-management occurred smoothly after liberation. However, the structure of the laws that were passed was inherited from colonialist powers, precluding radical change. In the second case, these rarely developed into broader participatory and self-management movements. Thus, in these cases there were not substantial changes. More important changes came from the countries where participation and self-management were employed as fundamental tenets of development after liberation. In Algeria, Peru, Tanzania and Yugoslavia, the introduction of self-management and participation considerably altered the existing path of development. On the other hand, in Bolivia (COMIBOL) and Malta (Malta Drydocks), workers' participation did not have such an impressive debut. Only after a long and difficult struggle by the unions in two of the most important

firms in their respective economies was this new form of production introduced. In Costa Rica and Mexico, participation spread, especially in agriculture, and in agricultural cooperatives. Only the broadest concept of workers' participation and self-management is accepted in Bangladesh and Guyana where no clear formulation of institutions has been made.

In many cases, the progressive parties which fought for liberation supported the idea of participation and self-management, and used political means to introduce it — similar situation existed in Sri Lanka, Mexico and Malta. However, implementation of participation and self-management was not as widespread in these cases because the political parties in power changed very often — conservative parties suppressed participation and self-management while progressive parties supported them. Some of the constituencies which supported participation and self-management were progressive unions as in Bolivia, Malta and some military governments as in Peru. But most often, progressive governments, parties and unions were connected to these ideas.

Political factors are the main motivation of proponents of participation and self-management as they guarantee independent socioeconomic development, eliminate exploitative means of production, educate people, change social structures, decrease alienation in the workplace and develop political democracy. When the political motives for establishing participation and self-management were clearly defined as in Algeria, Peru, Tanzania and Yugoslavia, the actualization of these goals took place on a larger scale. Socio-technical theory and job redesign as well as the Human Relations Approach are the basis for participation and self-management in those countries which derive their political motivation from the Philosophy of Industrial Peace as in Bangladesh, Costa Rica, India, Malta, Peru and Sri Lanka.

There are four classifications of the degree of participation and self-management in the countries studied. First, there are those countries where participation and self-management were introduced into the whole economy and society. The highest degree of this was found in Yugoslavia, where it had spread throughout the entire social and economic structure. In Algeria, the model of cooperative self-management in agriculture and co-determination in the industrial sector were introduced. It is worthwhile mentioning that the state retained most decision-making rights. In the seventies, the Peruvian government implemented self-management and participation in the agricultural sector and industry. Tanzania focused on the agricultural sector in Ujamma villages, which includes 90% of the population. Second, in Bolivia and Malta, participation and self-management were introduced only in selected areas of the economy. Here, the most important enterprises of each of these countries were affected. However, in Mexico and Costa Rica, the agricultural sector was affected. The third group consists of those countries which embraced the Philosophy of Industrial Peace such as India, Sri Lanka and Zambia. The public sector is most affected by this scheme. In the fourth group, only the most elementary forms of participation have been introduced, as in Guyana and Bangladesh.

Classifying the countries studied according to the form of ownership which prevails in areas of participation and self-management, the following distinctions appear: Public Ownership, as in Algeria, Bangladesh, Guyana, India, Peru, Sri Lanka, Tanzania and Zambia; Private Ownership, as in Bangladesh, India, Malta and Zambia; Cooperative Ownership, as in Algeria, Bangladesh, Costa Rica, Mexico and Peru; and, Social Ownership, as in Peru and Yugoslavia.

Chronologically, in the sixties and seventies, participation and self-management grew rapidly; in the eighties, due to the varied crises in the developing countries, stagnant and more traditional policies proliferated.

The forms and institutions of decision-making in these countries are now presented. Yugoslav practice aims to promote workers' decision-making on all issues. Legal statutes define the procedures and institutions of the direct and indirect decision-making of workers. Co-determination, in which workers participate on the executive board of the firm while the manager is chosen by the government and supervises the Assembly of Workers, is exercised in Algeria. Three forms of workers' decision-making can be found in Peru: self-management in agricultural cooperatives; co-determination in labor communities in industry; and, self-management in the social sector. Organizational forms were adjusted to facilitate such decision-making. Decision-making in Tanzania is concentrated in the village communes, governed by the village community. The executive board of the village community is actually a workers' council. COMIBOL, in Bolivia, introduced a form of co-determination which includes worker's decision-making. Malta Drydocks implemented various self-managed bodies on the level of the entire enterprise and its subsidiary departments. Employee Coinfluence is an integral part of India's decision-making platform in which there is joint consultation of workers and management. The workers' council in Sri Lanka and Zambia performs the consulting role which is defined as employee consultation. Traditional producer cooperatives prevail in Costa Rica and Mexico while, in Bangladesh and Guyana, it is unclear what role workers should have in decision-making. Organizational schemes reflect the perceived role of workers' decision-making in these countries. The differences therefore reveal various beliefs about the degree of workers' participation and self-management that should be permitted.

3. It is important to observe the realized degree of participation and self-management in decision-making, instead of just the legal outline of the scope of such programs. It is therefore expected that the countries of the first group Algeria, Peru, Tanzania and Yugoslavia have a greater degree of participation because of their sophisticated legal structures.

In the first phase after the introduction of participation and self-management, the countries studied displayed some degree of economic success but could not maintain it. This raises the questions of how self-management and participation were started and operated in these countries. Moreover, it is difficult to find compatible indicators of socioeconomic development to understand the kind of global changes in social and economic structures which were generated by the introduction of these programs. Because it was impossible to isolate those factors which were directly responsible for the success of participation and self-management in decision-making from those which were not, we are not able to provide a conclusive answer regarding the impact of the realized degree of participation and self-management on socioeconomic change and overall economic development in the countries studied.

The emphasis of the study was therefore the comparison of case studies of individual firms. The research focused on two questions: How and to what degree do workers actually participate in decision-making in these firms? How efficient are these participatory firms?

4. According to three criteria: independence of the firm in decision-making, independence of subgroups within the firm; and, the distribution of power with respect

to decision-making, the results of our analysis show that there is a great divergence between theory and practice. This is valid for public firms and production cooperatives as well as for Yugoslav self-managed firms. Except for the Mexican cooperative, Cruz Azul, all other case studies reveal that external groups, such as government, political parties and local power structures have a large role in decision-making. We also found that subgroups are often subject to central authority. And, especially in public firms, they do not have substantial autonomy in decision-making. The distribution of power in decision-making in the firms reflects traditional management structures of public firms, except in some cases such as Cruz Azul and Deeder Cooperative Society. Often, decision-making groups of workers do not function as originally planned or do not have the power to do so. In Yugoslavia, the oligarchic model of the distribution of power in management determines how decisions are made.

There is a positive relationship between the formal and actual degree of participation and self-management, as in COMIBOL, BHEL, Sri Lanka Port Authority and ROP, Ltd.; that is, in cases where there is a low degree of participation and self-management permitted by law, a low degree of workers' participation follows. It was also found that the reason for lower workers' participation rests on the fact that workers' representatives do not fulfill their obligations properly, as in BHEL, The National Bank of Commerce and ROP, Ltd. Sometimes, workers do not even desire to participate in decision-making. In our sample, there are also firms and cooperatives from which one can conclude that workers actively participate in major decision-making, as in Malta Drydocks, Urafiki Textile Mill, Cruz Azul, Deeder Cooperative Society and Brewery Union.

An important role in decision-making processes, regardless of the characteristics and type of the firm in which such decisions are made, belongs to the management. To a certain extent, this reflects the institutional structure of management in public firms. The same applies to production cooperatives where the legal responsibility of management is comparatively low. How the process of decision-making in production cooperatives proceeds depends upon the degree of cooperation between managers and workers in the cooperatives, as can be seen in Deeder Cooperative Society and Grameen Bank. In Yugoslav firms, most decisions are made by managers in conjunction with external entities. However, managers are frequently relieved of their decision-making responsibility because workers supposedly make all decisions. Yet, the actual decision-making power of workers is lower than the laws permit.

Unions, in general, support the introduction of participation and self-management even though, in some of the public firms, militant unions have opposed such measures, as in BHEL and Sri Lanka Port Authority. The latter unions fear that these new programs threaten their role in the decision-making process because, their role was previously undefined. If, in the process of introducing worker's participation and self-management, unions drop their role of protecting workers' interests too quickly, workers may become unorganized in dealing with management, and thus lose their bargaining power. On the other hand, if unions advocate competitive behavior to acquire more members, the conflicts between unions can grow to such an extent that participation and self-management will never arise.

Workers' evaluations of participation and self-management vary from being very good, as in Malta Drydocks and Urafiki Textile Mill, Ltd. to being very bad, as in Contex and Sri Lanka Port Authority. Through time, workers' opinions about the actual working of participation and self-management also differ. Generally, it is obvious that in all public firms limited by institutional factors, the actual participation of workers does not go beyond mere consultation and discussion of workers' welfare. In Yugoslav firms and production cooperatives, where the potential for genuine participation and self-management is greatest, the key question remains: how to give the workers real influence in decision-making? Because in reality, workers have little say, the question arises about whether or not it would be more appropriate for them to accept a more traditional role, similar to that which unions have in developed market economies. The empirical findings point in this direction.

5. The analysis of the economic behavior of the firms studied can be summarized as follows: The impact of participation and self-management on productive efficiency varies across the firms. The studies on The Sri Lanka Port Authority, The National Bank of Commerce, Urafiki Textile Mill, Ltd. and ROP, Ltd. do not reveal major productivity changes after the introduction of participation and self-management. In COMIBOL and the Peruvian cooperative, Contex, productivity decreased after the introduction of self-management and participation. In the production cooperative, Cruz Azul, and Brewery Union, the introduction of participation and self-management led to positive changes in productivity. For other firms there is no appropriate data and one cannot make definite conclusions.

The results of the analysis show that these firms behave very inelastically with respect to employment when a change in market parameters occurs.This concerns the employment of new workers under situations of expanding demand such as when the firm opts to hire seasonal workers instead of admitting new workers into the cooperative or when it opts to increase the number of overtime hours worked by existing members. In the case of decreasing demand, they decrease the number of hours worked of all members or simply allow some members to leave the cooperative. The security of employment is the most highly valued object of workers. Consequently, the efficiency of the self-managed and participatory firms may be endangered. In some cases, job security is a result of soft budget constraints in acquiring capital, financial irresponsibility and oligopolistic or monopolistic power of the firms as can be seen in public firms and Yugoslav firms. Consequently major distortions in the economy and losses in national income result from allocational and productive inefficiencies.

In other cases, a firm operates under a hard budget constraint, as in Cruz Azul and Coope-Silencio. Rigidity in employment does not have a major effect in this situation.

The data confirm three hypotheses about the basic differences between the remuneration of workers in capitalist, cooperative and self-managed firms.

Participatory or self-managed firms develop distributional schemes which not only include the direct payment of workers for work done (wages), but also include bonuses, various allowances and different forms of collective consumption. This is true for public firms, production cooperatives and Yugoslav firms.

Two characteristics are prominent regarding the internal distribution of income. The majority of these firms use some form of profit-sharing to distribute net income between workers. The distribution of income in these firms is much more egalitarian (and monetarily less) than that offered in capitalist firms. The bonus formula in SUNACOB ranges from 1 to 10% of individual productivity. In Cruz Azul, the system of capital accounts, known from the Mondragon Cooperatives, is employed. Workers are given three types of current income: basic wages; interest on individual capital accounts; and, bonuses, allowances and collective consumption. In Brewery Union, workers are paid a basic wage plus a bonus, based on individual productivity, as well as a bonus based on collective efficiency (5.7% of the income of the average worker in 1982). Past work was also taken into consideration, but it was done in a way which gave rise to the payment of larger bonuses to senior members. The range of wages varied in these firms. In Cruz Azul it was 1:24; at Brewery Union it was 1:2 in 1965. This raises the question of how motivation is affected especially in the example of Yugoslav firms.

The Yugoslav experience supports the thesis that different wages for equal work in different firms is more pronounced in the Yugoslav economy than it is in a capitalistic economy due to the absence of a labor market. Nevertheless, one cannot simply blame the absence of a labor market for all of these troubles; institutional factors and administrative restrictions of the Yugoslav economy permit firms to obtain monopolistic and oligopolistic rents. However, allowing firms to have complete freedom in deciding how much to pay their workers and managers will lead to even greater pay differences between firms, due to the lack of a real labor market. This signifies that the existence of labor markets is a necessary requirement for the efficient working of the Yugoslav economy.

Financing these firms is the major problem associated with their efficient operation. On the basis of the data, we came to the following conclusions:

First, almost all of the public firms, some of the cooperative firms and all of the Yugoslav firms studied are larger than their capitalist counterparts. The explanation for this rests on the proliferation of soft budget constraints in acquiring capital and the tendency of preserving employment.

Second, the use of capital accounts in production cooperatives is a good way of financing, as seen in Cruz Azul. Another way is to adopt a scheme to stimulate the necessary saving by members, as in Coope Silencio, or to discourage current consumption, as in Deeder Cooperative Society.

Third, from the Yugoslav case it is evident that in order to achieve economic efficiency and guarantee democratic decision-making, it is important to establish conditions for a direct transfer of savings into stocks within primary capital markets, and for their mobility within secondary capital markets. The introduction of primary and secondary capital markets in order to permit participation in decision-making in firms as well as to distribute profit and risk over a broader base is deemed necessary.

6. The introduction of participation and self-management in developing countries is not on a one way path towards total realization. Instead, it is characterized by huge oscillations. In this context, there is no simple formula to employ for all developing countries. Experience shows that when a country explicitly wishes to adopt workers' participation and self-management as a goal of development, no single decree can guarantee its success. Progressive political parties, once in power, made this mistake. The events in Algeria, Peru, Tanzania and Yugoslavia reflect this fact. In Yugoslavia, even though the ideology of self-management and participation prevailed for many years, all of the ramifications of the pure model of self-management have been exhausted. The pure model of self-management must be replaced by one which provides higher economic efficiency in practice. This can be achieved only by introducing competition among different types of enterprises, where advantages of participatory firms will be shown, of course, if they really exist.

REFERENCES

Abel, P. (1983): "The Viability of Industrial Producer Cooperation," in F. Heller et al. *Industrial Yearbook of Organizational Democracy, I*:73-107.

Adisez, I (1969): "Odnosi izmedu organa upravljanja i organa rukovodenja," *Glediste, X(4)*, 535-550.

Alchian, A. and Harold Demsetz (1972): "Production, Information Costs, and Economic Organization", *American Economic Review 62*, 777-795.

Aoki, M. (1982): "Equilibrium Growth of the Hierarchical Firm; Shareholder-Employee Cooperative Game Approach," *American Economic Review*, 72, 1097-1110.

Arzensek, V. (1974): "Legitimnost managementa: pokusaj institucionalne in koncesualne analyze," *Biblioteka: Covjek i sistem*, Zagreb.

Barkai, H. (1977): *Growth Patterns of the Kibutz Economy*, Amsterdam, North Holland.

Ben-Ner, A. (1982): "Changing Values and Preferences in Communal Organizations: Econometric Evidence from the Experince of the Israeli Kibbutz," in Jones and Svejnar, *Participatory Self-managed Firms: Evaluating Economic Performance*.

Bernstein, P. (1982): "Necessary Elements for Effective Worker Participation in Decision-Making," in Lindenfeld, Rotschild - Whitt, *Workplace Democracy and Social Change*, 51-85.

Blumberg, P. (1973): *Industrial Democracy, The Sociology of Participation*, New York, Schocken Books.

Bonin, J. (1984): "Membership and Employment in an Egalitarian Cooperative," *Economica 51*, 295-305.

________(1985): "Labor Management and Capital Maintenance: Investment Decisions in the Socialist Labor-Managed Firm," *Advances in the Economic Analysis of Participatory and Labor-Managed Firms,* Greenwich, CT: JAI Press, I.

Bonin, J. and L. Putterman (1986): "Economics of Cooperation and the Labor-Managed Economy," Brown University, Working Paper No. 86-4.

Bradley, K. and A. Gelb (1982): "The Mondragon Cooperatives: Guidelines for a Cooperative Economy," in Derek Jones, Jan Svejnar, *Participatory and Self-Managed Firms: Evaluating Economic Performance*, Cambridge: Lexington Press.

Bradley, M. and S. Smith (1987): "On Illyrian Macroeconomics," *Economica*.

Brus, W, (1975): *Socialist Ownership and Political Systems*, London, Routledge & Kegan Paul.

Cable, J. and F. FitzRoy (1980): "Productive Efficiency, Incentives and Employee Participation: Some Preliminary Results for West Germany," *Kyklos 33*, 100-121.

Clarke, Fachett, Roberts (1972): *Workers' Participation in Managament in Britain*, London, Heinemann.

Clegg, S. (1983): "Organizational Democracy, Power and Participation" in F. Heller et al. *International Yearbook of Organizational Democracy, I.*

Conte, M. (1982): "Participation and Performance in U.S. Labor-Managed Firms, in Derek Jones, Jan Svejnar, *Participatory and Self-Managed Firms; Evaluating Economic Performance*, Cambridge: Lexington Press.

Crouch, C. (1983): "Introduction to Volume I," in F. Heller et al. *International Yearbook of Organizational Democracy, I.*

Defourny, J. (1986): "Une analyse financiere comparative de travailleurs et des enterprises capitalistes in France" *Annals of Public and Cooperative Economy*, 57(1), 55-78.

Defourny, J., S. Estrin and D. Jones (1985): "*The Effects of Worker Participation on Enterprise Performance: Empirical Evidence from French Cooperatives,*" 3, 197-217.

Domar, E. (1966): "The Soviet Collective Farm as a Producers" Cooperative, *American Economic Review 57*, 347-373.

Dow, G. (1983): "Labor Management in Competitive Society," Institut for Social and Policy Studies, Working Paper, No. 10008, Yale University.

Dreze, J. (1976): "Some Theory of Labor Management and Participation," *Econometrica 44*, 1125-139.

Elliot, J. (1985): *Comperative Economic System*, Wardsworth Publishing Company, Belmont: California.

Ellerman, D. (1984): "Theory of Legal Structure: Worker Cooperatives," *Journal of Economics* 18, 861- 891.

Estrin, S. (1983): *Self-Management: Economic Theory and Yugoslav Practice*, Cambridge, Cambridge: University Press.

________(1985): "The Role of Producer Co-ops in Employment Creation," *Economic Analysis and Workers' Participation,*" 19, 345-382.

Estrin, S., D. Jones and J. Svejnar (1987): "The Productivity Effects of Worker Participation: Producer Cooperatives in Western Economies," *Journal of Comparative Economics* 11, 40-61.

Estrin, S., J. Svejnar and R. Moore (1988): "Market Imperfection, Labor Management and Earnings Differentials in a Developing Economy: Theory and Econometric Evidence from Yugoslavia," *Quarterly Journal of Economics*.

Furobotn, E. and S. Pejovich (1970): "Property Rights and the Behavior of the Firm in a Socialist State: The Example of Yugoslavia," *Zeitschrift fur Nationalekonomie,*" 431-454.

Furobotn, E. (1979): "Bank Credit and the Labor-Managed Firm: The Yugoslav Case," in Eric Furobotn, Svetozar Pejovich, *The Economics of Property Rights*, Cambridge: 257-276.

Garson, D. (1977): *Worker Self-Management in Industry: The West European Experience,* Praeger, New York.

Glas, M. (1986): "Monograph in the Economic Issues," Ljubljana, ICPE (unpublished).

________ (1988): "Urejanje podrocja razdelitve in uveljavljanja trznih zakonitosti," in *Kaj storiti za bolj trzno gospodarstvo*, Ljubljana, GZS.

Goldstein, S. (1985): *Prijedlog* 85, Zagreb, Scientia Yugoslavica.

Gomulka, S. (1982): "Macroeconomic Reserves, Constraints and Systemic Factors in the Dynamics of the Polish Crisis 1980-1982," *Yearbook of East European Economics.*

Gui, B. (1984): "Basque versus Illyrian Labor-Managed Firm: The Problem of Property Rights," *Journal of Comparative Economics*, 8, 168-181.

_______(1985): "Limits to External Financing: A Model and an Application to Labor-Managed Firms," *Advances in the Economic Analysis of Participatory and Labor-Managed Firms*, I, 107-120.

_______(1987): "Investment Decisions in a Worker Managed Firm," *Economic Analysis and Workers' Management*, 3.

Gunn, C. (1984): *Workers Self Management in the United States*, Ithaca, Cornell Press.

Hammer, T., R. Stern and M. Gurdon (1982): "Workers' Ownership and Attitudes Towards Participation," in Frank Lindenfeld, Joyce Rotschild-Whitt, *Workplace Democracy and Social Changes*, 87-109.

Horvat, B. (1982): *Politicka ekonomija socijalizma*, Zagreb, Globus.

_______ (1983): The World Economy from the Socialist View Point, *Economic Analysis and Workers' Management*, XVII, 1.

_______ (1986): "Farewell to the Illyrian Firm," *Economic Analysis and Workers' Management.*

ILO, (1969): Participation of Workers in Decision-making within Undertakings, Geneve, *Labour Management* 33.

Ireland, N. and P. Law (1982): *The Economics of Labor Managed Enterprises*, New York: St. Martin's Press.

Jensen, M. and W. Meckling (1979): "Rights and Production Functions: An Application to Labor-Managed Firms and Codetermination," *Journal of Business* 52, 469-506.

Johnson, A. and W. Whyte (1977): "The Mondragon System of Worker Production Cooperatives," *Industrial and Labor Relations Review*, 31(1).

Jones, D. (1976): "British Economic Thought and Associations of Labourers," *Annals of Public and Cooperative Economy* 47, 1-32.

_______(1979): " U.S. Producer Cooperatives: The Record to Date," *Industrial Relations*, 18, 342-357.

_______(1980): "Producer Cooperatives in Industrialized Western Economies," *Brit. J. Ind. Relations* 18, 141-154.

_______(1982): "British Producer Cooperatives 1948-1968: Productivity and Organizational Structure," in Derek Jones, Jan Svejnar, *Participatory and Self-Managed Firms: Evaluating Economic Performance*, Cambridge.

_______(1985): "The Cooperative Sector and Dualism in Command Economies: Theory and Evidence for the Case of Poland" *Advances in the Economic Analysis of Participatory and Labor-Managed Firms*, I, 195-218.

_______(1987): "The Effects of Worker Participation on Productivity in Command Economies: Evidence for the Case of Polish Producer Cooperatives," Hamilton College (unpublished).

Jones, D. and D. Backus (1977): "British Producer Cooperatives in the Footwear Industry: An Empirical Test of the Theory of Financing," *Economic Journal* 87, 488-510.

Jones, D. and J. Svejnar (1982): *Participatory and Self-Managed Firms: Evaluating Economic Performance,* Cambridge.

________(1985): "Participation, Profit Sharing, Worker Ownership and Efficiency in Italian Producer Cooperatives, *Economica*, 52, 449-465.

Kavcic, B. (1983): "Guidelines for the Elaboration of Case Studies in Yugoslavia, ICPE (unpublished).

________(1986): " Workers' Participation and Self-Management: The Sociological Approach," Ljubljana, ICPE, (unpublished).

Kester, G. and H. Thomas (1983): "Partial and Gradual Transition to Workers' Self-Management," in *Workers' Self-Management and Participation in Developing Countries*, Ljubljana, ICPE.

Kornai, J. (1984): "Comments on Papers Prepared in the World Bank about Socialist Countries," Washington, World Bank.

Likert, R. (1961): *New Patterns of Management*, New York, McGraw-Hill.

Lindenfeld, F. and J. Rothschild-Whitt (1982): *Workplace Democracy and Social Change*, Boston, Porter Sargent Publishers, Inc..

McCain, R. (1977): "On the Optimal Financial Environment for Worker Cooperatives," *Zeitschrift fur Nationalekonomie*, 37, 355-384.

________(1980): "A Theory of Codetermination," *Zeitschrift fur Nationalekonomie*, 40, 355-384.

McClintock, C. (1984): Podesta Bruno, Schurrah Martin, "Latin American Promises and Failures: Peru and Chile," in Frank Heller et al. *International Yearbook of Organizational Democracy*, Vol. II, 443-473.

Meade, J. (1972): " The Theory of Labour-Managed Firms and of Profit-Sharing," *Economic Journal* 82, 402-428.

Mgyin, N. (1987): "Are Self-managed Firms efficient? The Experience of Danish Fully and Partly Self-managed Firms," *Advances in the Economic Analysis of Participatory and Labor Managed Firms*, 2, JAI Press, Greenwich.

Miovic, P. (1975): "Determinants of Income Differentials in Yugoslav Self-Managed Enterprises," Ph.D. Dissertation, University of Pennslyvania.

Mitchel, J. (1987): "Credit Rationing, Budget Softness and Salaries in Yugoslav Firms," University of Southern California, (unpublished).

Miyazaki, H. (1984): "Internal Bargaining, Labor Contracts, and a Marshallian Theory of the Firm," *American Economic Review* 74 (1984), 381-393.

Montias, J. M. (1976: *The Structure of Economic Systems*, New Haven, Yale University Press.

Mugendi, N. (1987): " Workers' Participation and Self- Management for Development: its Politics in Comparative Perspectives," Ljubljana, ICPE.

Nuti, M. (1988), "On Ward-Vanek Cooperatives and James Meade's Labour-Capital Discriminating Partnerships," European University Institute, Florence, (unpublished).

Oakeshott, R. (1973): "Mondragon: Spain Oasis of Democracy," *Observer*, January 23, 1973 and Jaroslav Vanek (Ed) *Self-Management: Economic Liberation of Man*, Harward, Penguin.

Obradovic, J. (1975): "Participacija: rezultati istrazivanja i teoretski modeli," *Biblioteka: Covjek i sistem*, Zagreb.

Ohman, B. (1983): "The Debate on Wage-Earner Funds in Scandinavia," in Frank Heller et al. *International Yearbook of Organizational Democracy*, I, 35-53.

Perotin, V. (1986): "Conditions of Survival and Closure of French Worker Cooperatives: Some Preliminary Findings," *Advances in the Economic Analysis of Participatory and Labor Managed Firms*, 1.

Petrin, T. (1981): "Analiza vzrokov koncentracije organizacijskih enot v industriji in v trgovini Jugoslavije v letih 1954-1978, doktorska dizertacija, Ljubljana.

Prasnikar, J. (1983): *Teorija i praksa organizacije udruzenog rada*, Zagreb, CEKADE.

________(1990): "Routes of privatization of socialist economies - a case of Yugoslavia," University of Pittsburgh, unpublished.

Prasnikar, J. and V. Prasnikar (1986): "The Yugoslav Self-managed Firm in Historical Perspective," *Economic and Industrial Democracy*, 7, 167-190.2

Prasnikar, J. and J. Svejnar (1988): "Enterprise Behavior in Yugoslavia," *Advances in the Economic Analysis of Participatory and Labor-Managed Firms* 3.

Prasnikar, V. (1987): "Are Hours and Workers Separate Inputs in Yugoslav Self-Managed Firms," University of Pittsburgh (unpublished).

Pryor, F. (1983): "The Economics of Production Cooperatives: A Reader's Guide," *Annals of Public and Co-operative Economy*, 133-172.

________(1987): "Development Strategy, Growth, and Income Distribution in Poor Countries: Malawi and Madagascar," Swarthmore College (unpublished).

Pucko, D. (1986): "Bolj razcisceni odnosi med temeljnimi, delovnimi in sestavljenimi organizacijami-pogoj za vecjo ucinkovitost gospodarjenja," Zbornik *Samoupravljanje in ekonomska ucinkovitost*, Ekonomska fakulteta Borisa Kidrica Ljubljana, 377-390.

Putterman, L. (1984): "Agricultural Co-operation and Village Democracy in Tanzania," in Frank Heller et al. *International Yearbook of Organizational Democracy*, II 473-495.

Ribnikar, I. (1989): Uvod v financno ekonomijo, Ljubljana, Pegaz.

Ross, S. (1974): " On the Economic Theory of Agency and the Principle of Similarity," v M.S. Balch, D.L. McFadden in S.Y. Wu eds. *Essays on Economic Behavior Under Uncertainty*, Amsterdam, North Holland.

Rothschild-Whitt, J. (1982): "The Collectivist Organization: An Alternative to Bureaucratic Models," in Frank Lindenfeld, Rothschild-Whitt, *Workplace Democracy and Social Change*, 23-51.

Sen, A. (1966): "Labour Allocation in a Cooperative Enterprise," *Review of Economic Studies*, Vol. XXXIII, 351-371.

Sen, A. (1977): " Rational Fools: A Critique of the Behavioral Foundations of Economic Theory," *Philosophy and Public Affairs* 6, 317-344.

Sertel, M. (1982): *Workers and Incentives*, Amsterdam, North Holland.

Sethi, K. (1986): " Workers' Self-Management & Participation and Structure and Process of Work Organizations & Industrial Relations," Ljubljana, ICPE. (unpublished).

Sethi, K. and J. Mankindy (1983): "Workers' Self-Management and Participation in Developing Countries - A Comparative Analysis," in *Workers' Self-Management and Participation in Developing Countries*, Ljubljana, ICPE.

Sibille, H. (1982): "Les cooperative ouvrieres de production en France et dans le CEE," *Notes et Etudes Documentaires*, No. 4690-91, La Documentation Francaise, Paris.

Spinnewyn, F. and J. Svejnar (1990): "Optimal Membership, Employment and Income Distribution in Unionized, Participatory and Labor Managed Firms," forthcoming in *Journal of Labor Economics.*

Stephen, F. (1978): "Bank Credit and Investment by the Yugoslav Firm," *Ekonomska analiza*, 3-4, 149-167.

Stambuk, V. (1986): "Filozofsko-socioloski aspekti samoupravljanja in participacije," Ljubljana, ICPE (unpublished).

Steinherr, A. and J. F. Thisse (1979): "Are Labor-Managers Really Perverse?," *Economic Letters* 2, 137-142.

Streeck, W. (1984): "Co-determination: The Fourth Decade," in Frank Heller et al. *International Yearbook of Organizational Democracy*, II, 391-425.

Svejnar, J. (1982a): "On the theory of a participatory firm," *Journal of Economic Theory,* 27(2) 313-330.

________(1982b), "Codetermination and Productivity: Empirical Evidence from the Federal Republic of Germany," in Derek Jones, Jan Svejnar, *Participatory and Self-Managed Firms Evaluating Economic Performance*, Cambridge, Lexington Press.

Taylor, F. (1947): *Scientific Management*, New York, Harper & Row.

Teulings, W. (1984), "The Social, Cultural and Political Setting of Industrial Democracy," in Frank Heller et al. *International Yearbook of Organizational Democracy*, II, 233-261.

Thomas, H. C. Logan (1980): *Mondragon: An Economic Analysis*, London. George Allen and Unwin.

Thurley, K. (1984): "Comparative Studies of Industrial Democracy in an Organizational Perspective," in Frank Heller et al, *International Yearbook of Organizational Democracy*, II, 171-183.

Tyson, L. (1977): "A Permanent Income Hypothesis for the Yugoslav Firm," *Economica* 44, 393-408.

Vahcic, A. (1982): "Neka metodoloska pitanja merenja uticaja samoupravljanja i ucesca radnika u odlucivanju na drustveni napredak i ekonomske promene," ICPE (unpublished).

Vahcic, A. and T. Petrin (1986): "Economics of Self-Management, Self-Managed Enterprises and Public Enterprises", *Public Enterprise*, 6(2).

________(1987): "Financial System for Restructuring the Yugoslav Economy", European University Institute, Florence.

Vahcic, A., J. Prasnikar and T. Petrin (1988): "Development Strategy of the Commune of Yugoslavia for the Period 1988-1989. A Search for Enterpreneours in a Self-Managed Economy," IV. International Conference on Self-management and Participation, Vienna.

Vanek, J. (1970): *The General Theory of Labor-Managed Market Economies*, Ithaca, Cornell University Press.

________ (1971): *The Participatory Economy*, Ithaca, Cornell University Press.

________ (1975): *Self-Management, Economic Liberation of Man*, Baltimore, Penguin.

________ (1977): *The Labor-Managed Economy: Essays by Jaroslav Vanek*, Ithaca, Cornell University Press.

________ (1984): "The Praxis of Popular Participation in the Development Process," Cornell University (unpublished).

________ (1987): "Towards a Just, Efficient and Fully Democratic Society," *Advances in the Economic Analysis of Participatory and Labor-Managed Firms*, 2.

Ward, B. (1958): "The Firm in Illyria: Market Syndicalism," *American Economic Review* 68, 566-589.

_______(1967): *The Socialist Economy: A Study of Organizational Alternatives*, New York: Random House.

Warner, M. (1984): "Organizational Democracy - The History of an Idea," in Frank Heller et al. *International Yearbook of Organizational Democracy* 2.

Webb, S. and B. Webb (1920): *The Socialist Economy: A Study of Organizational Alternatives*, New York, Random House.

Weber, M. (1947): *The Theory of Social and Economic Organization*, New York, Oxford University Press.

Wild, R. (1976): *Work Organization: A Study of Manual Work and Mass Production*, London, John Wiley and Sons.

Williamson, O. (1980): "The Organization of Work: A Comparative Institutional Assessment," *Journal of Economic Behaviour and Organization* 1, 5-38.

Zafiris, N. (1982): "Appropriability Rules, Capital Maintenance, and the Efficiency of Cooperative Investment, *Journal of Comparative Economics* 6 55-75.

Zevi, A. (1982): "The Performance of Italian Producer Cooperatives," in Derek Jones, Jan Svejnar, *Participatory and Self-Managed Firms: Evaluating Economic Performance*, Cambridge, Lexington Press.

Zupanov, J. (1969): "O problemima upravljanja i ruukovodenja u radnoj organizaciji, *Ekonomske studije, br. 7.*

________ (1986): "Problemi razgranicevanja samoupravljacke i poslovodne funkcije s aspekta ekonomske efikasnosti," in Zbornik *Samoupravljanje in ekonomska ucinkovitost*, Ljubljana, Ekonomska fakulteta, Ljubljana, 415-427.

SOURCES

Avendano J et al. (ed.), 1980, Workers' Self-Management and Participation, National Reports Vol. I (Bangladesh, Malta, Peru, Yugoslavia), Ljubljana, ICPE.

Avendano J et al. (ed.), 1981, Workers' Self-Management and Participation, National Reports Vol. II (Algeria, Guyana, India, Tanzania), Ljubljana, ICPE.

Vahcic Ales, Smole-Grobovsek Vesna, 1983, Workers' Self-Management and Participation, National Reports Vol. III (Costa Rica, Sri Lanka, Zambia), Ljubljana, ICPE.

Vahcic Ales, Smole-Grobovsek Vesna, 1983, Workers' Self-Managament and Participation in Practice (Case studies from Bolivia, Malta, India, Zambia), Ljubljana, ICPE.

Vahcic Ales, Smole-Grobovsek Vesna, 1983, Workers' Self-Management and Participation in Practice (Case studies from Bangladesh, Costa Rica, Mexico, Peru).

Sethi Kristan et al., 1983, Workers' Self-Management and Participation in Developing Countries, Comparative Analysis and Recent Developments.

Grozdanic Stanislav, 1984, "Case Study on the Motor Works Rakovica-Belgrade" (unpublished).

Nedkov et al., 1984, "A Case Study of the Work Organization Alumina" (unpublished).

Prasnikar et.al., 1986, "A Case Study of the Union Brewery Ljubljana" (unpublished).

INDEX

Abel, P., 13, 17, 20
absenteeism, 5
Adisez, I., 129
African Socialism, 30, 46, 47
agricultural cooperatives, 49, 136, 137
Alchian, A., 132
Algeria, 13, 19, 25, 26, 33, 34, 36, 44-47, 49, 66, 71, 82, 101, 128, 136-137, 140
  General Assembly, 49
  FLN, 26
  Le Gestion Socialiste des Enterprises, 26
  Workers' Assembly, 49
alienation, 6
allocation of capital, 11
allowances, 116
Alumina, 67-68, 73, 84, 86, 91, 93, 98, 99, 101, 108, 119
  Workers' Assembly, 91
  Workers' Council, 91
American cooperatives, 22
Argentina, 25
Arusha Declaration, 41
Arzensek, V., 130
Austria, 14

Backus, D., 22
Bangladesh, 25, 26, 33-36, 45, 50, 66-68, 72, 83-84, 97, 101, 107-108, 136-137
  Awami league, 23
  Industrial Disputes Act, 23, 36
  Labor Policy Statment, 36, 45
bankruptcy, 13
bargaining, 8, 134
Ben Ner, A., 8
Bernstein, P., 4, 5
BHEL, 69-69, 74, 79, 86-87, 93, 95, 100, 102, 104, 111-112, 116, 120-121, 123, 128-129, 131-133, 138
  Bhopal unit (HEIL), 69, 80, 95, 100, 104, 116, 128, 131-132
  Hardware Divison (HEEP), 69, 80, 95, 100, 104, 117, 128, 131-132
  Joint Committees, 87, 93 104
Blumberg, P. 19
Bolivian government, 35
Bolivia, 25, 27, 33, 34, 37, 44-45, 47, 66, 68-69, 79, 95, 100, 104, 128, 130, 135-136
Bonin, J., 8, 9, 20
bonus, 5, 116, 121 139
bonus system, 121
Bradley, K. 22
Bradley, M., 11
Brewery Union, 67-68, 73-74, 85-86, 92-94, 98-99, 101, 103, 109-111, 114, 117, 120-124, 130-131, 133, 139
  basic organization of associated labor (BOAL), 92
  composite organization of associated labor (COAL), 92

Workers Assembly, 92
Workers Council, 92, 98
working organization, 92

Cable, J., 12, 16
capital accounts, 122
capital accumulation, 16
capital market, 10, 140
capitalism, 10, 15, 17
capitalist countries, 17
capitalist country, 15
capitalist economy, 140
capitalist firm, 4
capital-intensive technology, 111
China, 18
Clarke, F. R., 20
Clegg, S., 16
Codetermination Law, 21
codetermination, 4, 16, 21, 36, 37, 49, 56, 58, 64, 134, 136, 137
collective bargaining, 14
collective consumption, 6, 115, 121, 132, 139
collective needs, 6
collective workers' funds, 16
COMIBOL, 33, 35, 37, 44, 46, 51, 68-69, 74,79, 86-87, 93, 95, 100, 102-104, 111-112, 116, 120-131, 133, 135, 137-139
Administrative Council, 51, 87
Board of Directors, 51, 80, 87
Federation of Unionized MineWorkers (FJTMB), 4, 27
Production Boards, 51, 87
communist party, 18
conservative parties, 16
constant returns of scale, 11
Contex, 67, 72, 84, 91, 93-94, 97, 101, 103, 108, 129, 138
Administrative Council, 91
General Assembly, 91
Conte, M., 22
cooperation, 15
cooperative ownership, 136
cooperative firm, 7
cooperatives, 16
Coope-Silencio, 67, 72, 75, 84, 90, 93, 97, 101, 107, 111, 113, 120, 122-124, 126, 129, 131, 133, 139-140
Administrative Council, 83, 90, 97
General Assembly, 90
Managing Committee, 90
Costa Rica, 25, 27, 33-35, 37, 44-46, 2, 66-67, 72, 83, 97, 101, 107, 135-137
Land Settlement Law, 27, 37, 38
Law on Cooperative Associations, 27, 37, 38
Institute for Cooperative Development, 37
The Administrative Council, 52
The General Assembly, 52
The Institut for Cooperation (INFOCOOP), 52
Crouch, C., 16
Cruz Azul, 47-48, 67-68, 71, 75, 78, 83, 86, 89, 93-94, 96, 101, 103, 107, 110-111, 113-114, 118, 120, 122-125,128, 131, 133, 138-140
Administrative Council, 96
General Assembly, 89, 96, 107
Czechoslovakia, 18

Danish cooperatives, 22
Danish society, 16
Deeder Cooperative Society, 67-68, 72, 75, 84, 86, 90, 93-94, 97, 101, 103, 107, 111,113, 118, 120, 122, 124, 126, 128-129, 138, 140
Administrative Council, 90
General Assembly, 90
Defourney, J., 22
democratic enterprise, 5
Demsetz, H., 132
Denmark, 14
developed capitalist countries, 19
developing countries, 18, 19, 23, 66, 135

distributional schemes, 139
division of labor, 15
Domar, E. 7, 8, 103
Dreze, J., 10, 133

East Germany, 18
Economic Behavior, 110
economic development, 75, 135
economic efficiency, 5, 17, 18, 110
Economics of Self-Management, 6
economies of scale, 17
egalitarian distribution of income, 16
Elliot, J., 13
Emery, 19
employee coinfluence, 137
employment policy, 112, 113
employment stability, 134
employment, 110
England, 25
English cooperatives, 22
English cooperative, 12
entrepreneurship, 17
entry of enterprises, 11, 110, 127
Estrin, S., 8, 11, 17, 20, 21, 22, 131
European social democracy, 13
Europe, 111
external decision-makers, 76
external finance, 10
external shares, 133
externally finance, 17

Fatchett, 20
finance theory, 10
financing, 110
FitzRoy, F., 12, 16
fluctuation, 115
France, 14, 21
free-rider effect, 9
French cooperatives, 12, 13, 17, 22
functional participation, 133
Furobotn, E., 7, 9, 125, 134

Garson, J., 14
Gelb, A., 22
general equillibrium theory, 12
Gini inequality index, 123
Goldstein, S., 129
Gordon, M., 20
Grameen Bank, 67, 72, 84, 91, 93-94, 97, 101, 103, 108, 111, 128-131, 139
Great Britain, 21
Gui, B., 10, 20, 22, 126
Gunn, C., 22
Guyana, 28, 33-35, 37, 45-46, 53, 66, 136-137
  Guidelines of Workers Participation, 28
  People's Progressive Party, 28
  Public Corporations Act, 37, 38
  The Divisional Council, 53
  The Industrial Relations Board, 53
  The Workers' Council, 53
  The Workers-Management Participation, 53

Hammer, T.R., 20
hard budget constraint, 115
Herbst, 19
Hidalgo, 131
Higher Economic Associations, 43
Horvat, B., 8, 10, 11, 12, 16, 18, 20-24, 126, 129, 133-134
Human Relations Approach, 136
Human Relations Theory, 3, 35
Human Theory Approach, 4
Hungary, 18

Illyrian firm, 7
ILO (International Labor Office), 19
income for collective consumption, 76
income in kind, 77, 116
income, 110
India, 25, 28, 33-35, 44-46, 54, 66, 69, 79, 95, 100, 104, 120, 128, 136-137

Board of Directors, 54
Congress Party, 28
Industrial Disputes Act, 28, 39, 54
Joint Management Council, 38, 54
Joint Plan Council, 54
Shop Council, 54
Industrial Democracy, 3
industrial revolution, 13, 15
Industrial Sociology, 3
Industry of motors Rakovica, 67-68, 73, 85, 92-93, 98, 109, 119
Board of Directors, 92
Workers' Council, 92
internal distribution, 73
internal finance, 9, 10, 11
Ireland, N., 20
Israeli cooperative, 12
Italian cooperatives, 12, 17
Italy, 14, 21

Jensen, M., 132, 133
job security, 112
joint consultation, 137
joint managment-labor council, 14
Jones, D., 21, 22

Karnataka, 128
Kaunda, 32
Kavcic, B., 20, 130
Keynesian macroeconomic theory, 12
Keynesian monetary theory, 11

labor-communities, 137
labor-managed firm, 4
labor market, 9
labor productivity, 110
Labour Policy Statement, 36
Lagunas, 131
Law, P., 20
liberation, 136
life-time employment, 134
Likert, R., 20

macroeconomic stability, 11
macroeconomics, 11
Madagaskar, 22
Malawi, 22
Malta 25, 29, 33-35, 39, 44-45, 47, 54, 66, 68, 70, 80, 95, 100, 105, 128, 135-136
General Workers Union, 29, 47
Labour Party of Malta, 29, 54, 63
Management Committees, 63
Marsa Shipyard, 47
Villa Rossa Hotel, 47
Malta Drydocks, 33, 39, 44, 46-47, 54, 56, 68, 70, 74, 80, 86-87, 93-95, 100, 102-103, 105, 110, 112, 117, 123, 128-129, 131, 133-135, 137-138
Board of the enterprise, 87
Workers Council, 56, 87
General Workers' Union, 100
Joint Consultative Committe, 54
Port Workers Ordinance, 54
Maltese shipbuilding, 47
management, 94
market concentration, 112
Marx, K. 22
Maslow, 3
Maya, E., 19
McCain, R., 11, 16, 21
Meade, J., 7, 8, 123
Meckling, W., 132, 133
Meidner Plan, 16, 21
members account, 122
Mexican Enterprises, 122
Mexican Law on Production Cooperatives, 125
Mexico, 25, 29, 33-35, 39, 44-47, 57, 66-68, 71, 83, 96, 101, 107, 110, 128, 130, 135-137
General Assembly, 57
General Law of Cooperative Societies, 29, 40, 57
Law on Cooperatives, 29
The Administrative Council, 57
microeconomics, 11
Mill, J.S., 22

Miovic, P., 134
Mitchel, J., 134
Miyazaki, M., 103
Mondragon cooperatives, 20, 139
Mondragon's system, 20, 126
Mondragon, 8, 10, 13, 17, 22, 64, 122, 130
monopolistic pressure, 114
Mygind, N., 22

National Bank of Commerce, 68, 70 81, 86, 88, 93, 96, 100-102, 105, 111, 117, 128-129, 132, 138-139
  Branch Executive Committee, 88
  Master Worker's Council, 88
  Regional Advisory Committee, 88
National Bank of Yugoslavia, 126
neoclassical enterprise, 124
neoclassical theory, 6
net income per worker, 7, 76, 77
net income, 139
Norway, 14, 21
Nuti, M., 127, 133-134
Nyrere, J., 30, 88

Obradovic, J.,130
Ohman, B., 21
oligopolistic pressure, 114

Pareto optimum, 123
Pejovich, S., 125, 134
Perotin, V., 21, 22
Peruvian government, 136
Peru, 13, 19, 25, 33-35, 40, 44-47, 58, 66-67, 72, 84, 98, 101, 108, 136-137, 140
  Abitration Council, 58
  Administrative Council, 58
  "basic" industry, 64
  Certificates of Social Purposes, 64
  Commune Council, 58
  Exucitive Committee, 58
  General Assembly, 58, 64
  General Law of Industries, 40, 128
  Industrial Bank of Peru, 64
  Labor Community, 58, 64
  Paid Corporate Fund, 63
  Social Property Law, 40
  social sector, 58
  Industrial Bank of Peru, 64
Petrin, T., 18, 129
Philosophy of Industrial Peace, 135, 136
physical productivity, 110
Poland, 18
political democracy, 15, 18
power-centered participation, 4
Prasnikar, J., 20, 64, 129, 130, 133, 134 Prasnikar, V., 64
private firms, 13
private investment, 17
private ownership, 136
producer cooperatives, 137
production cooperative, 4, 9, 17, 94, 113, 120, 124-125
production efficiency, 110
productivity, 110
profit sharing, 134, 139
profit, 4, 7
progressive parties, 13, 14, 16, 136, 140
progressive unions, 136
Pryor, F., 17, 20, 22, 67, 128
public enterprise, 94, 99, 102, 113, 120, 124, 125
public firms, 67, 138
public ownership, 136
Pucko, D., 129
pure model of self-management, 140
Putterman, L., 20, 64

quantity theory of money, 11

recruitment of members, 113
Republic of Macedonia, 133
Republic of Slovenia, 133
returns of scale, 111

revolutionary party, 23
Ribnikar, I., 134
Roberts, 20
ROP Limited, 68, 71, 81, 86, 89, 93, 96, 101-103, 106, 111, 120, 128-129, 131-132
  Board of Directors, 89
  Industrial Development Cooperation (INDECO), 82, 128, 131
  Party Committee, 89
  Workers Committees, 89, 101, 106
  Worker's Council, 89
Ross, S., 133

self-financing cooperatives, 17
self-managed democracy, 76, 77
self-managed national economy, 9
seniority rule, 134
Sen, A., 9, 20, 132
Sertel, M., 12, 121
Sibille, H., 22
Smith, S., 11
social property, 124
social sector, 137
social welfare, 3, 6
Socialist Countries, 18
socialist revolution, 13
socialist society, 18
socialization of capital, 16
socioeconomic systems, 135
Socio-technical Theory and Job Redesign, 3, 136
Socio-technical theory, 136
soft budget constraint, 115, 126
SONACOB, 71, 82, 86, 89, 96, 101, 106, 118, 121, 128-129
South American countries, 25
Soviet Union, 18
Spinnewyn, F., 8
Sri Lanka Ports Authority, 68, 70, 81, 86, 88, 95, 100, 102-103, 105, 111-112, 117, 128-129, 131, 138-139
  Workers' Councils, 88, 95, 105
  National Workers' Union, 100
Sri Lanka, 25, 29, 33-35, 41, 44-46, 59, 66, 68, 70, 81, 95, 100, 105, 128, 136-137
  Employee Council, Act 41, 59
  United Front Election Manifest, 29
  United Front, 33
  Workers Council, 59, 137
Stambuk, V., 19, 20
Steinherr, A., 8
Stephen, F., 10
Stern, B., 20
stock-financed cooperatives, 17
Streeck, W., 16
Svejnar, J., 8, 16, 20, 21, 22, 119, 130, 133-134
Sweden, 14, 21
Swedish cooperatives, 22
Swedish method, 47
  Swedish society, 16
Swedish unions, 21

Tanzania, 13, 19, 25, 30, 33-34, 41, 44-47, 60-61, 65-66, 68, 70-71, 82, 96, 100-101, 105-106, 128, 136-137, 140
  Board of Directors, 60
  Executive Committee, 60
  Security of Employment Act, 30
  Tanganyika African National Union, 30
  Ujamaa Villages, 30
  Village Assembly, 60
  Village Council, 60
  Workers Council, 60
Taylor, F., 19
Thisse, J.F., 8
Thordason, 22
Thorsrud, 19
Tyson, L., 134

ujamaa villages, 47, 136
unemployment, 14

unified trade union in Yugoslavia, 102
unions, 99, 101, 135, 143
Urafiki Textile Mill, Ltd., 68, 71, 82, 86, 89, 93, 96, 101- 103, 106, 111, 120, 128-129, 131-132, 138-139
  Workers' Council, 88
USA, 22
Vahcic, A., 18, 129, 130
Vanek, J., 7, 8, 11, 12, 20, 21, 103, 121, 127
Velasco, J. A., 40, 44, 47
village communes, 137

Ward's model, 7
Ward, B., 7, 103, 123, 127
Warner, M., 21
Webb S. and B,, 21
Weber, M., 19
welfare benefits, 116
welfare, 4
West Germany, 14, 16, 21,
Westerm European firms, 123
Western countries, 15
Western European social democratic party, 13
Western Europe, 22, 124
Wild, 19
Williamson, O., 121, 132
workers shares, 133
workers' cooperatives, 67
workers' partnership, 127
workers' welfare, 75, 76, 77
worker-capital discriminatory partnership, 127
worker-managed firm, 4
Works Costitutions Act, 21
work-centered participation, 4

Yasin, 90
Yugoslav economy, 12, 126, 127, 133, 140
Yugoslav enterprise, 64, 67, 74, 78, 86, 93, 94, 99, 102, 103, 111, 112, 114, 120, 124, 126, 130, 134
Yugoslav firms, 20, 129, 139, 140
Yugoslav self-managed enterprise, 115, 124
Yugoslav self-managed firms, 74, 137
Yugoslavia, 8, 10, 13, 19, 25, 31, 33-35, 42, 44-47, 60, 66, 73, 84-85, 98-99, 101, 108-109, 123, 130, 134, 136-138, 140
  Basic Organizations of Associated Labor (BOAL), 44, 45, 60, 62, 91, 109, 130
  Communist Party, 31
  Constitution, 62
  Constitutional Amendment, 65
  The Law of Enterprises, 65
  Law of Associated Labor, 62
  working organization, 91, 101

Zafiris, N., 10
Zambia, 25, 32-34, 43-46, 63, 66, 71, 82, 96, 101, 106, 128, 136-137
  board of directors, 63
  Department of Industrial Participatory Democracy, 43-44, 96
  Industrial Relations Act, 32, 43, 63
  Philosophy of Humanism, 32
  Philosophy of Industrial Peace, 96
  United National Independence Party, 32
Zevi, A., 22
Zupanov, J., 129-130